See You in the Morning

There's a Season for Everything

By
Sharon Stephenson-Wilkerson

World rights reserved. This book or any portion thereof may not be copied or reproduced in any form or manner whatever, except as provided by law, without the written permission of the publisher, except by a reviewer who may quote brief passages in a review.

This book is sold with the understanding that the publisher is not engaged in giving spiritual, legal, medical, or other professional advice. If authoritative advice is needed, the reader should seek the counsel of a competent professional.

Copyright © 2013 ASPECT Books
ISBN-13: 978-1-4796-0022-9 (Paperback)
ISBN-13: 978-1-4796-0023-6 (ePub)
ISBN-13: 978-1-4796-0024-3 (Kindle)
Library of Congress Control Number: 2012922584

Published by

www.ASPECTBooks.com

Dedication

To my children—Kerrie, Stevie, and Mark—May you come to know your earthly father a little better through the reading of these pages and also your heavenly Father. Love, Mom

"Do you not know? Have you not heard? The Lord is the everlasting God, the Creator of the ends of the earth. He will not grow tired or weary, and His understanding no one can fathom" (Isa. 40:28, NIV).

"For My thoughts are not your thoughts, nor are your ways My ways," declares the Lord. "For as the heavens are higher than the earth, so are My ways higher than your ways, and My thoughts than your thoughts" (Isa. 55:8, 9).

Table of Contents

Dedication
iii

Foreword
vii

Introduction
ix

Preface
xi

Chapter One: There's a Time to be Born
15

Chapter Two: The One I Love
25

Chapter Three: He is My Shepherd
30

Chapter Four: Maker of All Things
37

Chapter Five: Heir of All Things
48

Chapter Six: The Author of Our Faith
59

Chapter Seven: "I Am"
71

Chapter Eight: My Strength
88

Chapter Nine: Light of the Morning
110

Foreword

In 1974 I accepted an invitation to become the pastor of the First Baptist Church in Rio Vista, Texas. This congregation has had the privilege of being led by some of the most gifted Southern Baptist Bible teachers and preachers—Dr. W. T. Conner; Dr. E. Leslie Carlson; Dr. Jesse Northcutt; and Dr. Leon McBeth. I served this congregation for three years (1974–77) while worked on a doctoral degree at Southwestern Baptist Theological Seminary in Fort Worth, Texas.

When I moved to Rio Vista, I met Sharon Stephenson. She played the piano at church, and I remember her not only as a talented musician but as a serious student of Scripture. I recall conversations we would have after the conclusion of the worship service regarding the content of the message. She often requested clarification or engaged me in dialogue.

Sharon and I have had two quite memorable telephone conversations. Both came "out of the blue." The first one came late in the evening on Friday, February 18, 1977, when she called to tell me that her husband Wally had been involved in a motorcycle accident, of which he did not survive. During the next few days and over the next several months, I attempted to minister to and support Sharon and her children during this devastating time.

The second call came on Saturday morning, August 11, 2001. Sharon caught me up on the last twenty years of her life. She related to me how God had been at work in her life. She also declared that she had decided to share her personal experiences in writing as an encouragement to others. She asked me to write the foreword to her book. I was honored to do so.

I believe that you will find this book to be a source of both information and inspiration. It contains tender reflections and honest, tough questions. One of the texts I used at Wally's memorial service was Psalm 121. The poet declares that he will look to the hills from which the help of God will come. Sharon Stephenson-Wilkerson's testimony is that through difficult circumstances she has looked to God. He has been the source of her faith and strength.

Dr. Ron Lyles, PhD,
Pastor, South Main Baptist Church
Pasadena, Texas

Introduction

The days are long, but the nights even longer. Each object that belongs to him becomes so painful to see and to touch. His slippers sit by his favorite chair; his glasses are on the table as if he has just walked away for a moment. Each room speaks of him—his presence is everywhere. Blessed memories, yet torment. There appears to be no relief in sight from this piercing, stabbing knife as it cuts deep into the heart. How she aches to change the course of time, but humans can only accept—not change. She cries copiously. There is bitterness in the tears, and little emotional release. *Where is God during this trial?* she asks again and again in her mind. He had preached at so many funerals and had brought comfort to many with his words of God's peace beyond understanding. But where was this peace for her now?

"Why, God, why did it have to end this way?" she wails in the form of a prayer. Anger creeps into her heart—a strange kind of anger—at him. How could he have left her, as if he had a choice? How silly she thought to be angry with him. She shakes her head back and forth while her hands are clasped over her face—tears dropping heavily to the floor. There are way too many emotions to deal with. Emotions she can't even begin to understand. The world is so ugly—the colors have faded. Nothing feels normal. Will this aching in her heart ever end?

I recently read about a woman whose husband had been a pastor for more than forty years. They were eagerly preparing for their fiftieth wedding anniversary. Suddenly, without warning he died after a short unexpected illness. When he died she had no idea how to find God on her own initiative. She was forced to realize that she had never made a decision for Christ on her own but had completely depended on her husband's faith. She was confused, lost, and bewildered. After the loss she realized her faith had been a secondhand faith. God desired for her to know Him personally—as a friend as well as Lord. How many people have at some time in their lives been stunned into this realization?

Conversely, I, the author of this book, have always been intense, questioning everything that seemed to hold a key to life and reality—physical as well as spiritual. This book is not my search for God, but His involvement in my life. This drama presents an indelible true story of a personal triumph over a destructive and ravaging sudden death of a young husband. You will marvel at the outcome!

This account is a vibrant testimony to God's faithfulness and His love that is deeper than any human can fathom or words can express. As you read I hope you will experience our family's authentic love for each other and for God. I hope you will be able to identify with some part of our story, may it bring tears to your eyes and truth to your heart.

Preface

The decision to write these factual memoirs was irrevocably sealed as it became overwhelmingly obvious to me of how much God had altered significant episodes in my life. The following accounts reflect incidents forever transmuted because of God's intervention. I began this book at age fifty-three and have spent five years completing it. I retired from teaching second grade and devoted my time to preparing this manuscript for publication. My deepest desire has been to describe and teach what I've ascertained about God's character. Together we have forged through valleys and winding mountainous roads. These stories reveal God's acts in my life. They're about Him, not me. Left to my own devices they would communicate empty hopes and dreams. They are now distinct and exclusive, fashioned like a beautiful garment.

God chose the means and times in which I would suffer so as to demonstrate His loving character. Our suffering reveals His sovereignty over each circumstance. I have drawn from His deep well of love—a love that moves away the pall and weariness from our dark spirits.

There's been a deep longing in my heart to observe passion and vitality in God's chosen people. I've tired of the conventional mannerisms and the Laodicean lip service that is observed in most Christian churches. God's Spirit is dampened and impotent. Sleep-inducing sermons, prayers, and songs are offered, but they lack the dynamism and zestfulness that surely

God desires. For years I've detested the spiritual status quo. I've hated the apathy of God's people. Right or wrong I am excessive. There's never been an in-between for me. Oh, I've wandered away from God, but He never left me. My self-destructiveness and self-centeredness led me down wrong roads; He brought me back.

In college I learned something about myself. I enjoy writing. Please keep in mind this autobiography is the accomplishment of an educator and not an authentic, experienced author. Nonetheless, it comes complete with human fears, struggles, and countless tears. The content is what is amazing and not a distinct writing style. At times I've felt overwhelmed and inadequate in this monstrous endeavor. Please note: You need to read the book in its entirety. Hidden in the middle is a moving encounter with the God of this universe. It will amaze you; it has altered my life forever. As you continue to read, events become more mysterious and exceptional. God performed a symphony and created a masterpiece as each detail is exposed. My son, Stevie, is a brick mason. The brick lays on the ground at first, but he can already picture it on the house. He lays one brick at a time, and soon it is a magnum opus. Our days are constructed one brick at a time. When it is all said and done, the Master Builder has a true work of art.

I heard a preacher say once that if we are burdened in our heart for the needs of someone else, God placed that burden there. We're not even good enough to think that way. I didn't want to spend hours praying and worrying about others. But if He encumbers you with a burden for others, it will not go away. If He calls you to do something, you cannot alter that call. It will remain. The call God gives is not easy, but it is a privileged duty. When He saves someone you're praying for, it is a mountaintop experience like none other.

The following narration is my perception of how God has worked in my life. Only He has the complete and accurate account stored in His memory. My interpretation is often foggy and limited as humans tend to be. Nevertheless, with my limited and restricted information, the events are unexaggerated and unembellished.

The purpose of this book was to leave a legacy for my family concerning God's faithfulness to me. But this book has turned into a story that I hope will touch many. As you walk beside me, I hope you will learn that God is real. We see Him in the sunset and in the stars scattered like crystal dust across the night sky—or in the shadow of a flock of geese dimming the moon. God is portrayed in the dawn as the earth awakes. Nathaniel Hawthrone, a nineteenth century American writer and novelist, wrote, "Our Creator would never have made such lovely days and have given us the deep hearts to enjoy them, above and beyond all thought, unless we were meant to be immortal."

Corrie ten Boom, a Christian and Holocaust survivor, has recounted a conversation she had with her father who explained that God would help them through the war, which ravaged their country during World War II. They all lived with fear every moment of each day. He explained, "If you were taking a trip, Corrie, you would not need your ticket until you arrived at the station ready to board the train. At the very moment you need God's grace, it will be poured out on you—enough to see you through any circumstance." God's grace sustained her through many horrors of the concentration camp and the loss of her family.

I don't claim to know how God does His work or when He will complete it, but I attest to the fact that He has met my needs and is utterly dependable no matter which direction my circumstances have taken me. I leave you now with this thought as I begin a journey very precious to me—my life!

"But we have this treasure in earthen vessels, so that the surpassing greatness of the power will be of God and not from ourselves; we are afflicted in every way, but not crushed; perplexed, but not despairing; persecuted, but not forsaken; struck down, but not destroyed ... Therefore do not lose heart

… For momentary, light affliction is producing for us an eternal weight of glory far beyond all comparison, while we look not at the things which are seen, but at the things which are not seen; for the things which are seen are temporary, but the things which are not seen are eternal" (2 Cor. 4:7–18).

Chapter One

There's a Time to be Born

In Ecclesiastes 3 Solomon says there is a time to be born and a time to die, and it is the memento of a truly wise man. But there is an interval between these two times of infinite importance. Time is only lent to us, and we cannot be too diligent in it. It is precious, short, passing, uncertain, irrevocable when gone, and something for which we must one day be accountable for. What would we give for more time? The very last words of Queen Elizabeth I were "All my possessions for a moment of time." The moments of time are too short, but it is what life is made up of—it is the fabric of life.

Writing one's story is a healing art. Thinking about all the stories passed down through the ages about oneself and others and about writing them down has a way of making them eternal. A writer actually lives twice—in the moment and in retrospection. Erica Jong wrote in her book *Fear of Fifty: A Midlife Memoir*, "Memory is the crux of our humanity. Without memory we have no identities."

That is really why I am writing an autobiography. Telling ones story is remarkably rewarding and healthy. It is capable of healing wounds that are inflicted upon us as we interact in an endlessly changing world of people and ideas. I have written my life in small sketches, a little today, a little yesterday, as I can remember it. I remember things from my childhood and on through the years. Good events and unpleasant ones, for that is how life comes to us. I am letting you into my heart and soul, the part that has depth and substance. Revealing through experiences my values and intimate relationships with other people. Unveiling my heart and soul, words so easily trivialized, illuminating significant and powerful spirituality. Speech is temporary, but the written word is stronger and surer.

Sometimes writing about one's life can appear like an ambitious project—for certain egotistical. But this book is written with purpose, and that purpose is to illuminate God and His character through experiences and details. I am a character in the story, but the real hero is an unexplainable, worthy, loving God whose character is beyond anyone's imagination—words cannot adequately describe Him. This is my time upon this vast earth, and I wish to share it, leave it for others, and remember it. One day, probably without warning, my life will end. But a little piece of my time will be preserved.

Once upon a time, Avie Ethel (Adams) Hester raced to Saint Francis Hospital in Carlsbad, New Mexico, on March 17, 1944, at around 4 o'clock in the afternoon after nine agonizing months of pregnancy, giving birth to a tiny baby girl who weighed less than five pounds. This date just happens to be a well-known Irish holiday, Saint Patrick's Day. My father, Weldon Leo Hester, almost named me Patricia when he heard the nurses proclaiming up and down the hallways that another little Patricia had just entered the world. However, with the luck of the Irish, mother was awake enough to remind him that their new baby's name was to be Sharon, not Patricia.

Uncle Jack had written mother from Korea requesting that if the baby was a girl that she be named Sharon. Mother liked the name, and it was settled. Daddy was a bit rattled because I came into the world much faster than most babies, and the hospital staff was anxious about the delivery. When mother arrived, nurses frantically searched the hospital for a doctor. It was obvious this birth would be any minute. Nurses chased down a doctor while others demanded that mother not breathe. After total confusion the doctor entered the room, mother breathed, and I was ushered into the world. They were ecstatic with a girl, for my brother Lee was four years old, and they were excited to now have a boy and a girl.

The world had been peering anxiously over the precipice of war when Lee was born. By 1944 World War II still raged on. President Roosevelt had endeavored to remain neutral, but with the attack on Pearl Harbor on December 7, 1941, that became impossible. So America entered the war that lasted until 1945.

"You came out screaming and kicking, a feisty little thing," Mother told me, retelling with pride a the story of my birth, a story she told so often we both knew it by heart. "Daddy and I would put you to sleep in your bed, and midway into through the night you would scream and squawk until we placed you into our bed between us. I would try to snuggle up next to you, but those tiny little hands would consistently push me away. Once you were satisfied that you had acquired your way, you would peacefully fall back asleep."

When I was given the name Sharon, it bore no significance, but it was rare at the time. As I've matured I've often wondered if my name had special meaning to God. Jesus is often called the rose of Sharon in the Bible. This unusual rose is a lovely flower that grows in the desert in the Middle East among other rare plants. This vast barren region is called the Plain of Sharon, which is located near the Mediterranean Sea between Caesarea and Joppa.

My parents were far from perfect, but in my small young eyes, they were faultless. Daddy was special. He enjoyed planting a garden every year, and we spent lots of time outdoors pulling weeds out of the freshly tilled soil. I pulled few weeds but received gratification by playing in the dirt while allowing wet worms to slither through my tiny fingers. I'm my father's shadow. At the age of three Daddy and I walked to a nearby diner for pie and coffee. He told this story often as I grew up. As I wiggled on the stool beside him, I talked nonstop. Finally, realizing how much I had embellished I explained, "If I don't quit talking, I won't have anything to say tomorrow!" Somehow I don't believe I convinced my father that he could be so lucky. I was always quite verbal. I've always been a talker and would have been spared much grief if I could have embraced the quality of silence.

My father was a simple man who worked for the railroad for many years. We weren't an affluent family, but love thrived in our home. Each year Lee and I attended a school carnival. The world was a much safer place back then, so we went together without our parents. Traditionally, I purchased a delightful ten-inch doll in a sparkling array of clothing. Daddy would meet me at the doll booth at a certain time. This was the highlight of the evening for me.

One year I wandered back and forth to the doll booth, but my father did not come. I noticed most of the dolls had been purchased. Pretty soon my tears turned to loud sobs. Suddenly my father was kneeling beside me holding my hand and wiping away my tears with his handkerchief. My father, who was five foot, two inches looked eight foot tall to me. Everything suddenly seemed to be right with the world. We purchased a doll, and I knew I could always depend upon him.

One summer evening as Lee and I played a rough and rowdy game on the lawn, I broke my left arm—the bone completely snapped. Daddy remained close by me at the hospital, holding my arm as we waited for the doctor to arrive. My dad dissipated any fears I might have had. I knew mother was nearby, but my dad's eyes were what I saw each and every time something big happened.

Conversely, Mother always took us to church. During Vacation Bible School when I was about three, we marched into church in perfect little lines. My sense of hearing heightened as the pianist played the march that signified our entrance into the auditorium. I struggled to see her over the pew and thought to myself that one day I would play the piano too. I never tried to evaluate why I loved music so much; I simply accepted it. This is what children do. They don't analyze—they accept. One Christmas I received a toy piano. It was eight inches high and included a little over an octave of keys. I picked out a few tunes by ear and spent oodles of time trying to learn familiar songs.

After we moved from Carlsbad to Fort Worth, Texas, my father took a job down the street making about $4.00 per week. We had no car, no television, no telephone—only our house and the four of us. But we were always rich according to Mother who survived the Great Depression, so we took over her older home in Fort Worth. We had a home, food, and lots of love. I grew up feeling that my parents always had everything under control. My former years of school were at B. H. Carrol Elementary. Our schedule was art one day/music the next day. I loved music, but I had to keep it under wraps lest I get beat up during recess. All the others loved art day. I could never comprehend why I appeared different, but I kept my mouth shut and enjoyed school and friends.

It's odd as we walk through life how much time it takes to learn about ourselves. This truth is a baffling mystery. Centuries ago Plato said in two words simply, "Know thyself." After all, who do we spend more time with? As years pass we realize how long it takes us to comprehend our feelings, observe our deeds, and explore our character. Our true identity often eludes us, leaving us frustrated for we learn in increments. We consistently carve new roads, climb mountains, and forge valleys. Choices make or break us. Understanding comes little by little.

This I do know—God reshaped the person I could have been. He lifted me up from a life full of dark, confusing experiences to a spectacular and incredible walk in the light. I discovered that knowing myself was conquered when I came to believe in the One who made me and had a plan already arranged for my journey on this earth. Did my name have significance? I don't know. But my life has had great worth as God weaved His plan into it.

I experienced a great change in my life, but I didn't know the significance at the time it took place. During Vacation Bible School I received Jesus into my heart. I understood very little about what I had done, but I was growing. I was baptized when we moved our membership to Wichita Street Baptist Church one year later.

We lived two blocks from our church, and I was always there. At age thirteen, I attended an all night watch service on New Year's Eve. We played volleyball, ping-pong, sang songs, ate, and fellowshipped most of the evening. As the new year approached, the adults went into the auditorium to pray in the new year. I don't know why, but I went with them. Most of the teens did not.

I didn't understand prayer, but I'd grown up hearing lots of them. I wondered about the validity of this part of the Christian life. Just because you believe something doesn't make it true. I wanted to find out "for real" if prayer worked both ways. You talk—God listens. God talks—you listen. That night I made a resolution to talk to God every night during the following year. You can't know unless you give it a try, I reasoned. I was faithful, but my prayers I'm sure were simple. What did I have to pray about at thirteen? I had no idea I was beginning the most profound thing in my life. God, the Creator and Designer of the entire universe, was about to become my partner for life. I didn't know the unexplainable power source that was about to be made available to me.

He began to purposefully lay steppingstones along the way in my uneventful life that would come back to me later on and would be incredibly important.

I grew up in the late 1940s and early 1950s, and when Mother and Daddy announced we were going downtown to shop, it was an all-day event. It seemed we drove for hours. Who knows, maybe we did. There were no freeways. I wasn't a good traveler—motion sickness always came over me. So Daddy would ask Mother and I to sing along the way. We loved to harmonize various tunes. One favorite I remember was an old hymn titled "It Is Well with My Soul" by Horatio Spafford.

Mr. Spafford wrote the words to this classic hymn when his heart was deeply troubled. In the mid-1800s he lost his wife and two daughters when their ship went down as they traveled across the Atlantic Ocean. Later as he sailed to England across the same ocean to bring back the only daughter he had left alive, someone shared with him that the ship they were on was close to the exact spot where his family had met their demise. Standing on the deck that day, he was so overwhelmed as he passed over the area that he wrote down the following words:

"When peace like a river, attendeth my way, When sorrows like sea billows roll: whatever my lot, Thou has taught me to say, It is well, it is well, with my soul.

"Tho' Satan should buffet, tho trials should come, Let this blest assurance control, that Christ has regarded my helpless estate, and hath shed His own blood for my soul. It is well, it is well with my soul.

"And, Lord, haste the day when the faith shall be sight, the clouds be rolled back as a scroll, the trump shall resound and the Lord shall descend, even so, It is well, it is well with my soul."

Years later I played this song on the piano for my mother and father's funerals, which were four months apart. We are not together now, death has temporarily separated us, but one day we will sing this song again. Mother and I will harmonize while Daddy smiles and listens.

All too soon, I entered the perplexing, frustrating teen years. I've always been small so my body never matched my age. I looked forward to becoming an adult when I thought I would get that adult body—but it never happened. Again some things we just accept. However, my closest friend introduced me to a boy, and she and I and her boyfriend began running around together.

This boy came from a dysfunctional family and it affected our relationship big time. I was hit by the realization that not all families were like mine. Instantly, he became abnormally possessive of me and hit me on a few occasions. He verbally threatened to kill my family, and I found myself in a situation I didn't know how to deal with. A neighbor informed us that my boyfriend secretly watched our house, and on one occasion he cut his wrists while we spoke over the telephone. My dad made me hang up so he could immediately call for an ambulance. The longer I knew him, the worse each incident became.

I felt I had nowhere to turn but to God. So I began praying about the problem, and God took care of it. While I was at church one Sunday morning, my parents went and talked with his parents. They immediately ended the relationship. I had really poured my heart out to God—He heard and He answered. So each time I prayed I looked for an answer from God, especially serious problems, and He always changed things for the better. Even though my faith as a young Christian was small, He made huge differences in my life.

By age fourteen I was playing the piano for services and the youth choir. As time went by, I became involved in a variety of mission projects. We did a Vacation Bible School for a black community, which was quite interesting. I played a pump organ (not fun); I don't know which part of my body did more work, my feet or my fingers. The children couldn't get over how white we were. This took place around 1959, so it was a strange situation for us all.

In subsequent years I played the piano for many youth and children's camps. I would bunk with the adults, many of whom were missionaries. We had prayer every night, but I remember being so afraid to pray with all these adults. My prayer life was between me and God. Public prayer was a little too much for me. Around that time, I began to feel God tug at my heart to become a missionary, although I didn't know where, why, or how.

How quickly our lives can turn in another direction. I had no direct intention to push God aside, but I fell in love. On a blind date I met my children's father. It seemed right from the onset. He had blond hair, clear blue eyes, and although he was short, he was oh so cute. Wally Stephenson lived on the west side of Fort Worth many miles away. He rode two buses to get to my house as often as he could. I recall our first date as if it were yesterday. My friend had a date, but they had to talk Wally and me into going along. My parents said often that when our eyes met even they saw something spark. Three weeks later he was all I could think of day and night.

We dated for six months before he entered the Naval Air Corp. After boot camp he was stationed on Midway Island for eighteen months. The separation hit us hard. We wrote each other every day, and we each began a picture album of the other. The flame never went out; it only grew stronger. Mother and I sent him candy and cookies on special occasions. It was odd; we barely knew each other, yet the relationship was set in cement the first night we met.

While on Midway Island, he wrote me that he was flying to Alaska. He was excited about seeing some sensational scenery. A few days after I received this letter, we heard on television that a plane returning from Alaska had crashed on Midway Island. The following day Daddy purchased a newspaper to obtain more details on the crash. I barely made it through school that day. Time dragged—I was at its mercy. Finally home, Daddy and I began to read the article. My face was ashen. I trembled as I tried to read aloud. I couldn't finish, so my dad read the rest.

So much fear gripped my heart. What if his name were there? We weren't engaged, married, or anything. He was a part of our family in our hearts, but the navy wouldn't see it that way. He and his mom were angry at one another. We knew she would not call us. I didn't know how I would react to sudden bad news that he was gone. Meticulously Daddy and I read each name, slowly, one at a time, stopping occasionally as if we didn't know if either of us could persist. The room filled with an eerie apprehension as we solemnly read the names of these young men—men who gave their lives in the service of our country. They were someone's son, brother, husband, or sweetheart. Our spirits plummeted as we continued to read the long list. A deep, sick feeling came over me. At last we came to the end—his name was not there. I could barely breathe. I knew I would worry until his next letter came. The following day like clockwork a letter arrived. Wally explained that he had been scheduled to be on the plane, but plans had changed. He graphically informed us about the crash he had witnessed. More than twenty men had died in the fiery crash, many Wally knew well. For some reason God had spared him.

During Christmas break, 1961, Wally came home and gave me an engagement ring. His next tour was Seattle, Washington, on an aircraft carrier, the U.S.S. Kearsarge, which was in dry dock. He called me almost every night, blowing what little money he had. Even though we were apart, our relationship blossomed. But our courtship would witness many problems in subsequent years for while words are sweet, actions speak louder.

We planned our wedding for June 15, 1962, which was right after I was scheduled to graduate from high school and a little after Wally had been in the navy for two years.

Chapter Two

The One I Love

It has been said that the three most beautiful words in any language are "I love you." The Bible claims that God is the epitome of love. I can attest to the fact that love can make all things work, for love never fails. As I reflect upon a scene some thirty-nine years ago, I am reminded of an old, old, song titled "The Little Church in the Wildwood." This church was my home away from home. One could even say I grew up here, for it was my second home for many years.

My church was a small neighborhood sanctuary only two blocks from my residence. The auditorium was only two or three years old—very sophisticated and magnificent. It was plush and had that smell of newness and fresh flowers. The carpet was a deep burgundy in contrast to the white walls with large stately white pillars down each aisle. The pews were covered with the same impressive color. The piano was a new, black baby grand; the organ was brand new as well. Both had a crisp, bright sound.

Years ago my family had joined this congregation. We had met in the old church building, which was also right down the road from our home. The building was small and had wooden floors that made irritating, creaky noises every time someone moved. The piano was an old upright, and the organ was small and limited to only a few variations of sounds.

As a church family we had all been excited when we moved into our new building. I remember the very first Sunday morning in the new church—no one made a sound. People spoke in a whisper. It was as if the building didn't yet belong to us.

The new church was only a few years old when Wally and I were married in it. For our special day, flowers and candles were set in place, preparing the splendid sanctuary for a small but formal wedding. There were family and friends gathered to witness this joyous event. The evening was hot, but Wally and I were more than ready to exchange vows.

The groom was late—many years later I discovered that this flaw in his character was ongoing. I slipped the beautiful, white gown over my head. It was a size 1, taken up to be a size 0. It featured an abundance of lace and a full skirt with a hoop to make it stand out. Mother helped me get ready, and Vanda Nance, my maid-of-honor, quietly slipped a penny in my shoe for good luck.

As we prepared for this special event, my Aunt Addie Lee walked in with a small tissue in her hand, her eyes red and swollen. After a few moments she spoke. "Oh, Sharon, you're just too little to be getting married!" She shared in a whimpering voice. I stared at her with no answer. It dampened my spirit a bit. Well, we all know now that if I'd waited until I got big enough to get married I would have been an old maid for sure.

Nevertheless, I couldn't wait to walk down the aisle. I was happy, young, and innocent. I'd dreamed of this day for two long years. Wally and I could now be together—the navy hopefully would not separate us again.

Pictures, stored neatly away today, indicate that the groom did show. He had everyone but me rattled. The church was ready. The organ played my pre-selected songs, and everyone was seated. Meanwhile, at the back of the auditorium Daddy and I gazed at one another. *Can I go through with this?* I thought. Nerves were beginning to show. *I wonder if I can grow a little bigger in a matter of minutes, because it's time.* Daddy froze.

"Daddy, let's go—it's time," I said nudging him. Finally he moved in step as we had been instructed to do.

The vows were exchanged and the next thing I knew the

preacher was saying, "You may kiss your bride." The music played a loud and pompous march proclaiming that the service was over. I was with the man of my dreams. We cautiously and slowly wove our way through the crowd to the getaway car with cans, paint, and shoe polish tied to the bumper, as friends ran alongside to cheer us onward.

Military life was unique and distinct. It took some doing for me to get used to it. We were stationed in Memphis, Tennessee, where Wally was learning about hydraulic systems on jet airplanes. My family visited on a vacation, and we all toured the Elvis Presley mansion. Elvis's uncle met us at the great wall surrounding the estate and took us up to the house in a pink jeep. It was quite dramatic—something we had not anticipated.

When we left Memphis, we moved to Beeville, Texas, where he put his newfound skills on airplanes to use at a base there. It was September, but it was very hot and muggy. I thought perhaps this was the entrance to hell itself. I'd never been so hot. It was difficult in this small town to find a house to rent. Wally kept returning to a little duplex that had a large sign in the backyard that had written on it "Stephenson's Grocery." He finally caught up with the landlords, and they became our surrogate parents. We learned over the next eighteen months to love them, and fortunately for us, they were deep, devoted Christians. One day Wally and I were taking a long walk with Mrs. Stephenson when she made a profound statement I'll never forget.

"You know, I've seen a lot of couples come and go in our rental houses, but I don't believe I've ever seen two people more in love. And I'm an old woman who's been around for a while and can spot it in a hurry."

I knew she was right on the money. We had married so young and were so far from home, but God had planted these beautiful people in our lives at a time when we needed stability and an older couple to look up to. I thank Him for that. Mr. Stephenson became Wally's best friend, and he even talked Wally into being baptized into the Baptist Church so we could go to church together. Wally went, but not often. It was a small step nonetheless.

God planted the Stephenson's in our lives when we needed them, but He also used us to help them. One day Mr. Stephenson died of a heart problem. I know it brought back painful memories to Wally because he lost his father at age fourteen in the same manner, but he was a big help to Mrs. Stephenson. Wally was no carpenter, but he began doing what he could to fix her apartments so she would be able to rent them in subsequent years. He rebuilt walls and did some wiring and painted—anything to make them more sturdy and durable—for she needed the income.

We left Beeville and entered the real world in August 1964. It was a cultural shock. But we moved to Fort Worth to be near our families and to find jobs and settle down. Wally loved my family dearly because all he had was his mom. He began calling my parent's mom and pop after our second date. A tad bit too soon to suit Daddy, but Mother loved it. To my parents he was not just my boyfriend, he wormed his way into their hearts and quickly became family. One could say he was their new son and another brother for my siblings, Lee, Susan, and Drew.

As the years rolled by, we began to notice that Wally was always in some kind of accident. Some mishap would occur on a consistent basis. My mom often commented: "I don't know how he's lived this long, Sharon. Nobody should have so many things happen to them in one lifetime. It's just not normal. Perhaps he places himself in too many predicaments he can't get out of or something. It's crazy." I know she worried about him just as I did.

But, on a different note, I visualized this as a positive attribute. It appeared to me he was capable of living life to the fullest—never afraid to try new things—while I believed I was a coward in comparison, always cautious and careful, not wanting to make mistakes. His attitude intrigued me. He was a daredevil, while I was negative, guarded, and reluctant in nature. I didn't know it at the time, but in the near future my perception of life would need to be very much like his—brave and strong.

Our union was ideal from the beginning, but remember, we didn't know each other very well. Our marriage was anything but tranquil and placid. Love between a man and a woman is a mystery known only to God. We loved each other, or we'd never have survived, but Wally's idea of marriage was that I was at home waiting for him whenever he saw fit to arrive. On the other hand, I wanted to do everything together. I saw no purpose in living life without him. So as the years went by, I became increasingly lonely and unhappy. But our love was our greatest bond, although sometimes it was our only bond.

Chapter Three

He is My Shepherd

If I were to paraphrase Psalm 23, this would be the main takeaway: He leads us day by day to the right places and in the right ways. He is the Shepherd, and we are His sheep.

Fortitude and determination were a way of life for Wally. In contrast, I found my resoluteness in God. Some people say that's a crutch and others claim it's the easy way. Just think about it—if a person is crippled they need crutches. God's Word says: "For the word of the cross is foolishness to those who are perishing, but to us who are being saved it is the power of God.... Where is the wise man? Where is the scribe? Where is the debater of this age? Has not God made foolish the wisdom of the world?" (1 Cor. 1:18, 20).

It is a fact that multitudes of people have chosen to leave Jesus on the cross and walk away. Because God allows us the freedom to willingly do this, the decision is up to each individual. God did not make puppets on a string. He never forces Himself on anyone—He does not pull the strings, moving us against our will. The first sermon ever preached about the cross puts all of humankind in a distinct position. Peter proclaimed this message: "Men of Israel, listen to these words: Jesus the Nazarene, a man attested to you by God to you by miracles and wonders and signs which God performed through Him in your midst, just as you yourselves know—this Man, delivered over by the predetermined plan and foreknowledge of God, you nailed to a cross by the hands of godless men and put

Him to death" (Acts 2:22, 23).

I had heard the story of Jesus dying on the cross for my sins when, and even before, I was nine years old. I knew I was not perfect and had an empty space in my heart that needed to be filled. I was raised in church and knew lots of church words, but to be honest, I didn't have a clue what they meant in real life. And I *knew* God even less. So it was a rude awakening when He began declaring Himself to me through an array of tragedies early in my life.

God wants to fill our lives with good things. He wants to give us hope, but we have to rely fully on Him. He desires a real relationship with us. Similar to parents' joy on Christmas morning when we see our children's eyes widen and brighten when they first see their presents, God gives what is needed and almost always more than is needed.

With great discomfort and confusion Wally continued putting his life in constant danger. Hesitantly, but obediently, I comforted him through each tragedy. But there was a pattern. He would get in a wreck or something and call me from the emergency room after the fact to say he was fine. Great or small I always fell apart.

One day it happened again. I got a call at work that he'd been in another wreck. But this one was bad. He had been involved in a head-on collision on our street. A young woman was driving her car up a steep incline, and as she approached our house, she and Wally had collided. His accelerator stuck, and he had to swerve to miss a parked oxygen truck. They crashed head-on. Wally was treated for deep lacerations to his left arm and for shock. The truck was totaled. I was crying my eyes out at work while he was laughing it all off. Providentially, he was not wearing a seatbelt, and he flew out the passenger's side of the truck and landed on the ground after totaling a tree in a neighbor's yard. But late that night he could not walk on his own. I placed kitchen chairs along the path to the bathroom so he could get there with my assistance.

Once again we made it through the crisis and moved on with life. But life was humdrum. We partied on the weekend with friends, but everything was monotonous, dull, and unproductive. Surprisingly my musical talent always kept me busy at church. Try as I might, I never understood why God always matched me up with churches that were in dire need of a pianist, but that kept me connected with a church.

Around this time we moved into his mom's house. She had married a man named Bob Lutz, and they had moved to bigger and better house in Arlington, so we took over her old place.

We soon approached another crossroad. Again something quite unusual happened to Wally. I was half asleep when he left the house to go to the ER to determine why he couldn't lay down and breathe at the same time. In my groggy state of mind I didn't think to go with him, but he called me at about 10:00 a.m. Only this time he wasn't laughing. He was in extreme pain, and he informed me they were about to hospitalize him.

"What's wrong?" I asked.

"Well, they think my right lung has collapsed. Will you pack me some things and bring them to the hospital?" He sounded tired and weak.

"How can someone's lung just collapse?" I asked frantically. I'd never heard of that.

"I don't know, but would you *please* hurry. I need you here now—can't talk about it." I held my head in my hands trying to grasp this new situation. *This could only happen to Wally*, I thought.

I hurried to All Saints Hospital and found his room. He'd had a spontaneous pneumothorax, meaning his lung had suddenly collapsed, and they don't know why. As a rule, this condition occurs in white, thin males in their early twenties. His smoking had not helped the situation, but he had a real good lung specialist coming to talk with him promptly. They would have to inflate the lung again through surgery, gluing his lung to the wall of the chest. He would be in the hospital for about three months.

I'd just started a new job as secretary for the James Avenue Baptist Church in Fort Worth. It was an extremely large and busy church, and my job was detailed and demanding. I worked all day and visited him every evening. But I was often the recipient of his bad moods at night because I hadn't been there during the day. He was tense, worried, and in constant pain. I tried to be patient. We didn't know it then, but this was a character-building period and a test of our love. In the back of my mind, I questioned whether Wally was a Christian. He said he was, but he acted awkward when we discussed it. He would put me down about it and immediately change the subject. This attitude made it hard for me to confirm it in my heart.

"Yes," he screamed one evening, "I'm a Christian. Would you leave me alone about it?" he said in an unkind manner. "Don't hound me about it. That makes me mad!"

"I only ask because I love you. I want us to be in heaven together someday, and I'd just like to be sure. I can't even discuss it with you without you coming all unglued."

"Leave it at yes, and leave it alone. I don't want to talk about it anymore." And that was that! He was very ill, but he didn't want to discuss anything important like living or dying.

When I entered the ICU directly after his surgery, they had him lying flat on his back. He kept screaming he was going to die if they didn't elevate the bed. His eyes were flaring, and he looked crazy. That's all I remember—I had to get out quickly. Fear gripped me. I just knew he might die, and I was still so concerned about where he would spend eternity. I loved him and wanted him to be with me in heaven. My concern was genuine and authentic. I simply wanted Wally and I on the same page. I cared about his salvation. His attitude toward spiritual matters never gave me any comfort.

He was hospitalized another two months and then released. He came straight home and began working on an old car—lighting those cigarettes up one by one. He was determined nothing would change his normal workload or his life.

The only thing that seemed to bother him was that he'd always wanted to live in the country. He was fearful that this might take away that dream. But in time he was his same positive self. He had been raised on a farm in Minnesota until he was about six before his family moved to Texas. His mom continued to encourage him to one day move to the country—she felt it was a good place to raise a family.

By now Wally and I had a growing concern as to why I'd never conceived. We had been married five years, and we were ready to start a family. We just assumed that it was naturally happen, but that didn't seem to be the case. It was suggested I have tests run to see why I couldn't get pregnant, but I hated anything to do with hospitals and doctors' offices, a fear I had had since the age of three. Nevertheless, God had a plan.

Wally had been back on his job about a week when he got a phone call that I was in the hospital. To my surprise, it was my appendix. It was almost gangrene and about to burst. Surgery was imminent. They removed it, and I stayed in the hospital for about a week. I shared a room with a lovely lady. She was married with children and lived in the country. She told me that deer ran in and out of their house all day. She cried on my shoulder often, for she missed her family so much. We became great friends. Each night we stood guard so we could go to the bathroom without turning on the nurse's light. We actually acted like a couple of kids doing this. She guarded for me and vice versa. We leaped over the railings and raced to the bathroom so not to be yelled at. I had so much fun in the hospital that momentarily I wasn't afraid of all the medical paraphernalia and staff.

This brief hospital stay gave me courage to see a doctor about having children, but I dreaded the tests as the time approached. I did my best to suck up my fears and be strong. Some of the tests were scary and painful. But when my doctor asked me to come to the hospital so he could run a dye into my fallopian tubes looking for any blockages, I freaked out.

"Call me a chicken or whatever you like, but I'm done and will not be back." He had also asked me to repeat a test, which went over like a led balloon. The test had made me nauseous and caused intense bleeding. I couldn't see me doing it again.

"I know this is not easy, but I consider you a very brave person to be doing what you're doing. So, I'll tell you what. This next test is the last. We will know for sure if any surgery will help you have even a ten percent chance of getting pregnant. You will be lightly sedated, so you will not know what's happening. How does that sound to you?" he asked.

He explained about the procedure in detail, assuring me that it would be the last, which was the main thing to me. I wanted a baby, so I decided to do whatever it took to get one.

I entered the hospital terrified and apprehensive. Old fears surfaced. Early that morning, however, a Christian neighbor asked if she could pray with me while I visited in her home. She sensed my uneasiness. After the prayer, I went home to play the piano, which always calmed my nerves. I began playing a tune I really liked but didn't recognize. God had the words come to mind right when I needed them. I knew God was presenting Himself to me and just for me as He always had done in the past. Jesus said, "My sheep hear me and know my voice." The words of the song comforted me:

"Day by day and with each passing moment, strength I find, to meet my trials here; trusting in my Father's wise bestowment, I've no cause for worry or for fear. He whose heart is kind beyond all measure gives unto each day what He deems best—lovingly, its part of pain and pleasure, mingling toil with peace and rest.

"Every day, the Lord Himself is near me with a special mercy for each hour; All my cares He fain would bear, and cheer me, He whose name is Counselor and Power; The protection of His child and treasure is a charge that on Himself He laid; "As thy days, thy strength shall be in measure," this the pledge to me He made."

The last verse is a prayer. God honors His pledges He makes to us until our lives on this earth are over, therefore, surely through all eternity. "Help me then in every tribulation so to trust Thy promises, O Lord, that I lose not faith's sweet consolation offered me within Thy holy Word. Help me, Lord, when toil and trouble meeting, ever to take, as from a father's hand, one by one, the days, the moments fleeting, till I reach the promised land."

I arrived at the hospital confident that God was with me. My doctor was marvelous and rare. He really cared. When I awoke Daddy and Elizabeth, my mother-in-law, were with me. I asked all sorts of questions and received blank stares in return. I thought something was wrong. I thought of cancer and all kinds of innuendoes. Late that evening mother called.

"Aren't you happy about the news?" she asked.

"What news? No one will tell me anything."

"We found out today you can't have a baby. Your tubes are completely clogged. But that's what you wanted to know. Now we can check on adoption. I'm so excited," she laughed.

Yes, I was elated. This was what we'd been trying to understand—which way to go. Now the direction was clear.

Dr. Tatum came into my room around 9:00 p.m., and as he shared the news, he looked down at the floor the entire time. He thought I'd be upset. When it became clear how excited we all were, he looked at me in a different manner.

"Well, I'll tell you what, Sharon. I'll write letters to any adoption agency you choose. Just let me know. I'm positive you'll be a great little mother. It takes more, you know, than just having a baby to be a mother. You're going to be a good one because you really want this career." He was so pleased that it ended so well. He left all smiles!

I was ecstatic at the possibilities that lay before me.

Chapter Four

Maker of All Things

Jesus desires to bless us, and everything that exists came into being through Him. We are His handiwork, too (Ps. 127: 3–5). This next stage of my life would test me in this area, but I had to trust that God knew the desires of my heart.

It quickly became apparent to Wally and me that adoption was going to be quite a task, but given some time and thought we decided we could figure it out. Wally worked long hours, so most of it was up to me.

Our first experience was unquestionably negative and almost harmful. Aunt Rene, my father's sister, sent us to the mayor of Irving. He told us it was all a matter of money. I'm sure we appeared to be the poorest people he'd ever dealt with. Well, Wally worked for General Dynamics as a flight line supervisor. He told us of one girl who had several couples desiring her baby. We'd have to pay for her upkeep, dental bills, and anything else she needed. We were more than astonished. That scenario was impossible for us. We drove home in silence. I was deeply depressed, but my mind kept thinking, *Where there's a will, there's a way.*

But a new day dawned, and my spirit improved. I decided to check the phone book and look for maternity homes. There were a select few. I telephoned several but found that Volunteers of America was the most upfront and friendly. The fee for everything was $980.00. Lawyers' fees and all. I made an appointment.

At our first appointment we met in a large room with seventy-five couples from all over the world. This home included a small nursery and delivery rooms. Women from nearby churches came over often and held the babies and rocked them. We met Mrs. Spock, the head supervisor, and had one appointment with her that incorporated the entire day. She matched her babies to each family, and she was very proud of her gift. As Wally and I left this long, exhausting meeting, our demeanor was anything but excited. She called us back into her office. "Please don't look so worried," she explained. "These interviews are very important concerning our selection of just the right child for you. In order to lift you a little, I want you to know your letter of approval is on the way. You are approved; so quit worrying. We'll get you that baby you want."

"So, does that mean we can get the ball rolling? Buy baby clothes and all that?" I screamed.

"Yes, you can! But no more worrying. The worst is over," she assured us. She put all our fears to rest that day.

Mother and I began shopping for baby clothes. I'd taken a job I knew I could leave when the call came. I worked for Kimball's Furniture Co. in the credit department as a switchboard operator. They knew I would leave the second I got the phone call. Dorothy, a colleague, and I were both expecting, but she was fat, and I weighed about 75 pounds. However, just for fun we had a shower together. When store clerks discovered mother and I were buying for a baby, they would jump right in and help us find cute little things. But they were confused at first when they took one look at me. As we explained they became even more excited than we were.

Fall whizzed around the corner and found us busy getting ready for the big event. We'd been told the baby might come around Christmas. But Christmas came and went and no little Stephenson. I told myself to stay busy, but nothing helped. My sister, Susan, was appalled when she viewed the nursery and saw I still had things in boxes. But I had hit rock bottom. Would it ever really happen? Most women experienced changes in their bodies—all I had was a letter. Christmas was Wednesday, by Thursday evening I fell to my knees. With tears dropping to the floor, I pleaded with God. I'd just left the nursery, shut the door, and determined not to go in again.

"I'm getting desperate, God. I don't know how I can go on waiting," I wailed. "I want the baby that You want to give me. Just help me wait. I turn my will over to You. You be in charge, and I will rest in that thought," I prayed confidently while my body shook with sobs.

It's odd how prayer affects a person. The problem still existed, but I released it to God. Something definitive happened to me. I went to work the next day with a big smile. God would work it out. I rested. In the New Testament Paul says that when we are weak, He is strong. My prayer was intense, and a peace swept over me.

Friday, three days after Christmas, Wally popped in and out of the store where I worked. He called me about every hour, checking to see if I could leave and did I have all the money for the baby. *What's up with this?* I thought. *He never bothers me at work.* I was pretty dense not to have suspected something, but unbeknownst to me he was at home busy making arrangements for our baby. Mrs. Spock had phoned him and told him we had a little girl and could pick her up around 5:00 p.m. He'd known since 9:00 in the morning. Finally he called.

"Are you ready for this?" He teased. "Are you sitting down? How would you feel about going and getting a little girl in about two hours?" he casually stated, trying to conceal his excitement.

It took a minute before it soaked in. I began jumping, yelling, and screaming. Pretty soon everyone was at the front pushing me to the door with shear joy. "Go get that baby!" they all told me. I don't even know how I drove home that afternoon. My mind was blown.

When I arrived home, Wally was hectically putting up the baby bed and getting the room ready.

"I can't believe I'm going to be a mother. No, I am a mother. Whatever! I'm twenty-five years old, and it's about time. My jobs gone—I'm retired."

For a moment we stopped everything and stared at one another. We hugged and cried. We were parents, and we loved each other so much. Besides our wedding day, nothing compared to this.

When we arrived at the home, Wally and I both paced the floor back and forth. I stopped for a moment and made a joke.

"Wait just a minute, I thought only the father did this part. Something's wrong here. We're running into each other in this small room." We both laughed. They brought Kerrie Lynette Stephenson in and placed her in my arms. Wally had only one thing to say.

"That's my daughter!" I still hear those words echoing down through the years. For a woman to accept someone else's child is not hard to comprehend. But for a man to love his wife when she cannot have his child and accept the responsibility of raising another's infant is amazing. I've heard many men at church who were fine men say they would never do that. Wally was an amazing man.

God knew what baby was for us. He knew the night I fell on my knees in prayer. God and I are connected together in a relationship. My friendship with God provides me with a sense of always resting in His providential care and guidance.

Today Kerrie is totally opposite from me, but very much like her father. Kerrie was meant for me, for God doesn't make mistakes. Our roles have changed. We are not just mother and daughter, but friends.

We began immediately planning to get her a brother or sister. Wally worked at General Dynamics, and I taught piano at home, making about $100 per week. Also, God found me a church that needed a piano player, not a surprise. We moved to Arlington to have a larger home, and I found myself very busy and happy.

Kerrie was two years old when we approached the same adoption agency about another child. We were placed on a waiting list and all was well. Wally had to go on a business trip to

Hartford, Connecticut, and planned be gone for about a month. He'd been there a week when I received another strange call. His other lung had collapsed, and he was hospitalized. He needed immediate surgery. But Wally didn't feel comfortable with this doctor, so he left the hospital against medical advice, but only after being warned his heart had been moved by his left lung, and he could have a heart problem flying home.

We picked him up at Love Field in Dallas late at night—he was whisked away in an ambulance. He'd had a few drinks with some cute stewardesses who were as surprised as him that an ambulance was taking him away. Their mouths dropped as the paramedics took control, but this gave Wally another interesting story he could tell later.

This surgery was just as dangerous as the first one, so once again I began to worry about if Wally had made things right with God. He had never given me sound assurance about his salvation. He avoided the issue completely. I pushed it on him, and he shoved it right back.

I loved Wally completely. I loved him body, soul, and spirit. But eternity is too long for anyone to be wrong! The morning of his surgery many people gathered in a small hospital room. I walked in and stood beside him, holding his hand. I immediately became his whipping post. His nerves were frayed, and the medications had altered his mood. He yelled rudely and demanded that I get up out of my chair and let someone else sit down. I wasn't even sitting; I was standing beside the bed holding his hand. On the verge of tears, I flung myself out of the room and into the hall. My mother followed.

"I want to be there for him, Mother, but there's nothing I can do. I feel so helpless," I explained between sobs.

"I know, and we both know he's trying to put on a good front in front of the others. You're the only one he can yell at, understand?"

"Mother, you of all people know how I've worried about Wally's salvation. I can't get him to talk to me about it at all."

"Sharon, I've told you before—don't worry about Wally. I never told you, but before he went into the navy, he brought me his confirmation papers and asked me to keep them in a safe place. They were real important to him. He's sincere about God—he just doesn't talk about it like you do," she explained. She managed to calm me down, but something still didn't feel right. Confirmation papers. What did that have to do with a relationship with Jesus?

The Bible is God's Holy Word to us. Jesus stated that a person must be born again in order to see the kingdom of heaven. It mentions nothing about a little piece of paper that some church made up to make people feel good about their souls. It is a conscious act, a decision to follow Jesus. It's not an act of man, but an act of God. No church can get anyone to heaven. When God forgives all your sins and makes you His child, that is a miracle greater than any other. Either God's way is the truth or we are all lost.

"If it's untrue then Christianity is a cruel hoax and one-third of the earth's people are victims of a foolish superstition, and we are all deceived, tricked, and the great pioneers of faith were nothing but fools—all of them—all captives of a beleaguering spirit. If they were not deceived, then it follows that the greatest folly in human history is to disbelieve and reject the words of Jesus" (Catherine Marshall, *A Man Called Peter*, p. 286).

It is a fact that you can be saved by Jesus and be completely confident of your salvation. "The one who believes in the Son of God has the testimony in himself; the one who does not believe God has made Him a liar, because he has not believed in the testimony that God has given concerning His Son. And the testimony is this, that God has given us eternal life, and this life is in His Son. He who has the Son has the life; he who does not have the Son of God does not have the life" (1 John 5:10–12).

Wally had received his early education at Holy Name, a Catholic school in Fort Worth, Texas, where he was taught about Jesus and how to be good and love others. His mother's intentions were good. But just because he understood who Jesus was, didn't mean it went to the heart. Wally believed in God. The New Testament informs us that the demons that encountered Jesus knew who He was. They even addressed Him as Lord. The Bible says that even though they recognize Jesus as the Son of God in the end they will be cast into the lake of fire mentioned in Revelation 20:14. Their *knowledge of Him* will not change things or alter their fate.

I heard an interesting true story about a missionary who was taking Bibles and Christian literature to a small town near Mexico City. To his surprise, the people were hungry for the knowledge of Jesus. After pastoring some small churches in America, he found their enthusiasm refreshing. There's so much apathy in America. For the most part many of these were Catholics, but they knew little of Jesus. As interpreters told them the good news, countless people were converted and saved. All accept one man who was the "fetcher." He would go and bring people to them, but he spoke little English. He kept pointing to his head and saying, "Jesus in my head." After several trips bringing friends to the missionaries, he approached the area with tears in his eyes, and a change had come over his face. He quietly looked into the eyes of one of the missionaries, unable to explain. He pointed to his head and then pointed to his heart. In broken English he did his best, "Jesus in my head, now Jesus in my heart." There is about a two-foot difference that will take one from the pits of hell to the splendor of heaven—from condemned to forgiven—from death to life.

Jesus says, "Behold, I stand at the door and knock; if anyone hears My voice and opens the door, I will come in to him and will dine with him, and he with Me" (Rev. 3:20).

During this time of pain and grief, I wanted assurance that Wally had accepted Jesus into his heart. This was no quest or an "I told you so" moment—I loved him and wanted to spend eternity with him. I wanted everyone I cared about to be in heaven one day. Wally was so inconsistent with his beliefs. He changed his message to match his audience, orienting the message to fit the circumstance.

Fortunately, Wally successfully made it through the surgery. He was soon back working at General Dynamics when a huge layoff took place. Soon he had no job. I telephoned the adoption home and was told by someone I didn't know that Wally had to have a job for at least a year before they would consider another adoption. Clearly, this was not good news. But Kerrie was only two and I knew I could spend lots of time with her—there were many things she and I could have fun doing together.

Overflowing with a certain amount of despair and disappointment, I again poured out my heart to God in prayer. "Okay, I'm not exactly pleased over this new development, but I asked you to give me the kids you wanted for me. So I will wait upon You. It if means a year or two, I'll wait." Again, God lifted the burden. I was determined to see it as the natural way of having children—sometimes people wait.

God always found a way for me to keep my focus on Him. Kerrie and I planned and implemented many diversions. And we had fun at whatever we found to do. Self-pity would creep in, and I would slam the door on it, keeping a positive attitude. Andre Crouch said it well in one of his songs: "If I'd never had a problem, I wouldn't know that God could solve'em."

King David wrote, "Behold, children are a gift of the Lord, the fruit of the womb is a reward. Like arrows in the hand of a warrior, so are the children of one's youth" (Ps. 127:3, 4).

Indescribable things happen to those who wait upon the Lord. He is committed to loving us, He is anxious to carry our burdens, and He enjoys giving us the desires of our heart (Ps. 37:4). To my surprise, two weeks after my call to the home the agency telephoned me. Only this time it was Mrs. Spock, the supervisor. Her call came around 10:00 in the morning. She explained that her time was limited, so she quickly blurted out the purpose of the call.

"We have this little baby boy, Mrs. Stephenson, and I was just wondering," she casually explained, "if you and your husband would possibly be interested in adopting him? You know how important it is for me to match the baby with the right parents. Well, I've been reviewing many files, there are at least fifty other couples ahead of ya'll, but every time I scan the portfolios, I keep returning to your file. This baby really should go to you if you want him. He matches you and your husband perfectly. I know it's short notice, but I just had to at least ask you."

Was I hearing all this correctly? It didn't seem possible. She said it all in such a calm manner. My response to her message was immediate, but I took nothing into consideration.

"Yes! We will take him!" I squealed, trying to be somewhat reserved, not ridiculous. She asked if we wanted to pick him up within the hour, if not, no one would be in the office again until 4:00 in the afternoon. She knew my response.

"We'll be there in one hour!" I could hear her laughing out loud at my reaction.

"I knew what you would say, how stupid of me. I don't know why I even asked," she said, still laughing. "See you in one hour." She hung up.

As for Wally, most men get woken up in the middle of the night with their wife screaming, "Honey, it's time." At least they had nine months to prepare. Here's how this went down.

"Get up! You're the father of a little boy! That's all I know, but he's ours if we want him," I shouted while doing a little jig beside the bed. I could barely get the words out. I sounded as if I'd just run a marathon—shallow breath and all. We both temporarily lost our minds. He tried to get dressed with me bumping into him. It was wild and crazy! We were in shock. It would have been a good movie scene. We stopped and looked at each other. "There's no grandmother around!" we shouted at the same time. "What should we do?" Suddenly it occurred to me that we had spent a lot of our savings when Wally lost his job. We didn't even have all the money we needed for this adoption. I made a fast call to my mother.

"You go get that baby," mother stated strongly. "We'll find a way to pay for him."

"That'll work," I screamed with excitement. "Mother, could you leave work and come over to help us?" I asked.

"I left five minutes ago," she remarked. "I'll bring your father for extra help." We called Elizabeth at her job, and she was dispatched immediately. The neighbor offered to watch Kerrie until we made it back home with her brother. The whole army was on the way!

Our only information on this baby was that he was skinny. I endeavored to picture a skinny baby. But when they brought him into the room in a small bassinette, he was little, cuddly, and cute. We gave him the full treatment when it came to the name, which was Wally's mom's idea. He became Walter Stewart Stephenson III—today he is my Stevie.

When we arrived home, it was a buzz of activity. Mother was washing dusty, stored baby bottles. Elizabeth was washing Kerrie's baby clothes. Daddy was actively engaged in putting up Kerrie's baby bed. I paused for a moment, glanced around, and my heart filled with ecstasy. *I'm so blessed to have this extended family*, I thought. *An excellent doctor said I'd never have a baby, but nothing is impossible with God! He also didn't make me wait years. Stevie is the only thing I ever won. Fifty other couples were waiting for him, but I got to have him.*

My life was like a fairy tale at the moment. I had it all—a wonderful family, children, a husband with a job, and work as the neighborhood piano teacher and at my church. My baby brother, Drew, bought our car and that paid for the adoption. Every detail fell into place.

As I focused intently at life, I thought it would never change. But life is one adjustment after another. Authentic peace and joy are intrinsic rather than extrinsic. Peace of mind is a relationship with our Creator.

Paul wrote about this theme in much of the New Testament.

In Philippians 4:11–13 he said, "Not that I speak from want, for I have learned to be content in whatever circumstances I am. I know how to get along with humble means, and I also know how to live in prosperity; in any and every circumstances I have learned the secret of being filled and going hungry, both of having abundance and suffering need. I can do all things through Him who strengthens me."

Chapter Five

Heir of All Things

Jesus has been exalted to be the firstborn heir of God. As we struggle to find our own identity and where we fit in, God's children must remember they belong to Jesus and, therefore, have an unlimited inheritance (Heb. 1:1–3).

It's odd how there are moments in our lives when we almost hold our breath hoping nothing will spoil or alter our happy state of affairs. I was so content I naively believed it might last forever. One day and out of the blue Wally made a monumental decision.

"Let's move to the country," he proclaimed as we sat around the kitchen table. "We're a family of four, and we need more space. Just think about it, Sharon. It'd be a great place to raise Kerrie and Stevie. They could have animals and room to play and grow. Country kids get to do lots more than city kids. Arlington is becoming a big city. Let's get out of here."

"We're growing just fine here, thank you very much." I crossed my arms as I stared at him and his ridiculous idea. "I'm perfectly happy. I don't want to leave. Don't rock the boat," I demanded.

"But, honey, the school would be small. Probably less chance of the kids being around drugs like city kids. It would be safer," he encouraged.

"I know, I know! You were raised on a farm in Minnesota, and you think all kids should grow up on a farm. But I faired just fine growing up in Fort Worth. It wasn't that bad! I turned out just fine, didn't I?"

"Just think about it. There are creeks to fish in; we can have cows and chickens. The kids will learn responsibilities in caring for them. Why, the airs even cleaner. Can't you see it my way for once?"

"Yes, I see your point. But I'm so happy here. Everything I need and enjoy is right here. Why would I want to leave?"

It was obvious we were not going to agree. His dream to live in the country was on the tip of his fingers. Everything seemed right. Wally and I had been paying on some land in a town called Rio Vista—a rural area about seven miles south of Cleburne, Texas—an insignificant town I never knew existed. Little did I know Wally wanted to relocate the whole family *now*!

We owned the land, and to make things worse, Mother and Daddy had already moved an old house there and spent most weekends working on it with Wally helping them often.

Consequently, he won the argument. I might have known. It was a real adjustment, mostly for me, after we made the big move. The kids now had tools, like hammers, nails, and screw guns to play with, for they were everywhere just for the taking. Other choices were boards and roofing supplies (both with nails protruding) and electric saws. The yard was full of stickers, bull nettles, and stinging nettles. Stevie was toddling, so he got the brunt of it. There was no cement, so they played in the mud. My life was turned upside down. You can take the girl out of the city, but you can't take the city out of the girl. Wally's dream was obviously not shared by me. The Baptist Church in town was small and closed up after Sunday services—nothing else went on during the week—it's a wonder they didn't board up the windows during the week.

However, in the country there were open meadows surrounded by beautiful woods, deep blue skies, and white fluffy clouds that didn't come from car motors. The sights, sounds, and smells were beyond words.

Black! I never knew it could be so black without city lights on street corners. I, out of boredom, went for a walk late one night.

When I turned onto the street, I couldn't see my hand in front of my face. It was scary. I quickly returned to the house.

Silence! You could feel it all around you. It was eerie. Even today if an ambulance comes down our road, we all notice and wonder if we know the person it's for.

A member of the Arlington church where I was pianist for three years became upset that I was leaving. She informed me she would write a letter to the First Baptist Church in Cleburne letting them know I was in the area. She tried to talk me into staying, but it was too late. Cleburne didn't need a pianist, but First Baptist Church Rio Vista did. Charles Lucas, the minister of music, after receiving a phone call concerning me, stopped by my home one Sunday afternoon with his son, Dale Lucas, and invited me to play the following Sunday. By the next Sunday night they wanted me to come back and be their pianist. I replaced Dale who went off to medical school to become a doctor.

I actually became the pianist for the town. I played for church, weddings, funerals, and anything the school needed me for. However, I wasn't as busy as in Arlington, and I gradually became lonely and filled with deep despair. I was not happy. I felt as if everything important in my life had been tossed aside—I felt rejected even by God. I later would discover God was in this all along.

The following true story illustrates how God cares about people who are barely aware of His existence. This authentic account is about a family who was blessed with a biblical certainty that could very well have reversed their lives if they had chosen life instead of death. We heard the words from a young, inexperienced preacher one day. God clearly gave this preacher the right words for this occasion. I'll never forget this experience.

The building was many years old, but loving hands had brushed layers of fresh, white paint on the timber in order to make it look as new as possible. The wood that made up the surrounding walls had been donated long ago when the old school was torn down. This quaint, conservative structure housed God's people in the little town of Rio Vista, Texas, in 1972.

On a cold, blustery winter day inside this small, country church, a tiny, inexpensive pine casket lay just in front of the altar—no blanket of flowers or anything. There were only a few cars in the minute gravel parking lot. Most of the family and friends had walked to the funeral, even though it was in the middle of winter and the wind howled furiously outside. The obsolete propane stoves were lit, but there was still a chill in the air. The wind seeped through tiny cracks in the walls of this old building, which was barely standing. No flowers surrounded the modest box, which was now the final abode for a precious little blond-headed boy who had just last week attended Rio Vista Elementary. Only a handful of mourners decorated the pews. They were unquestionably people of little wealth, and it was clearly a bleak day for a funeral.

I began the service by playing the appropriate funeral hymns with a deep desire to console. I was around twenty-eight years old and had played for only a few funerals. And this by far was the saddest of all. The preacher was young and inexperienced. He nodded for me to stop playing, and he reluctantly approached the pulpit. We both sought to offer peace to this small gathering. Perhaps he would accomplish this goal with a few words.

But what could he say? What words could anyone speak? This small boy had barely lived six years in this world, and most of them were dreary. He'd lived with a serious heart defect all his life. His parents had no monetary resources to correct it, which perhaps could have extended his life a little longer. This story drew many emotional responses as it circulated the town after his death. Teachers told how he would leave school each day to go home to eat lunch. He returned, however, hungry most days for lack of food in the home. No one knew or questioned. Regrettably, important things are often overlooked by people with high priorities.

I was curious about what the preacher would say. The situation was heartwrenching. The family was lost in their deep sorrow, and there was a great deal of crying in the small assembly.

"I would like to share with you a story from the Bible of a family who also lost their son, and in the midst of their grief, they asked a question," the preacher began.

"How will we ever see our child again? He is gone forever. Death has taken him away to never return again," he continued reading the Bible story. "Well, it so happened there was a wise man in the land who consoled them in their moment of grief with some astounding words of wisdom. This story is found in 2 Samuel 12."

I listened intensely. The preached continued. "You are right," the wise man explained. "You'll never see your son again here on this earth."

"But, there is a way for you to see him again!" The preacher stated clearly, precisely, slowly, and deliberately.

The congregation appeared puzzled as they gazed at one another, and all crying ceased. Slowly their swollen, red eyes filled with curiosity; they lifted their heads up and peered anxiously at this young man in the pulpit.

"Clearly, you know you can't bring your little boy back, but you can be reunited one day. The Bible gives us this hope. Jesus said, 'Let the little children come unto me … for such is the kingdom of heaven.' If you accept Jesus into your heart, you will be reunited with Jesus in heaven one day yourself. Then you will see your son again. There is hope beyond the grave," he concluded.

I watched as little by little hope began to stream into that room like a light shining brightly across the sanctuary. Everyone was touched, including me. I'd never heard that story before. I don't know what each individual did about Jesus that day, but I know the funeral began with despair and ended in triumph. Expectancy penetrated the dismal circumstance—hope in the midst of misfortune and loss. God is there when the water gets too high. He walks beside us through the fire, for He holds our hand.

Should a man see only power, he hunts and stalks, seeing what he can devour. His desire is to conquer and control. Like an animal, recognition is his prey—people are his prizes. Should a man look only inside himself, he becomes arrogant. His purpose is all that matters. He's controlled by his own desires—aspirations. Should a man seek after riches or education, he can never have enough. In the end he is left in want. In conclusion, I agree with the King Solomon who wrote Ecclesiastes—all is vanity.

God alone gives life purpose, especially in time, destiny, truth, and death. Consequently, as people looks into eternity, then and only then can they see a reason for their existence. We are made in God's image. We weren't made to walk apart from Him anymore than for a bird to walk or an elephant fly. When we walk with God, we gain purpose, resoluteness, and reason—even in death. When Jesus walked upon the earth, he demonstrated God's character. Love jumps barriers of color and race and is the only bow on life's dark cloud. It changes worthless things into joy. The greatest happiness is the conviction that we are loved for who we are.

As for me I experienced most of life in Rio Vista. My philosophies, ideologies, faith, and beliefs were tested to the brink. I look back now, and most situations were turned from failure to victory because God was in control. This is confirmed as you sink deeper into my story.

When Stevie was eleven months old we stayed in Mother and Daddy's unfinished house. Then Wally and I stupidly bought an old, stately house near Fort Worth and moved it down beside my parents' house to work on. We had to have all been a little crazy. We worked every minute anyone was not working their regular jobs, and I stayed home and raised the children. It got very lonely. After three years of this routine, an incredible sadness replaced all joy in my life.

 We had a huge picture window in our den that I often sat and stared out. I could see the cows, and I often thought of how much I'd become like them—put out to pasture. I became angry with everyone—even God. How could He do this to me? I tried. I asked my only neighbor who was about my age to sew clothes for me so we could get together and visit. She bluntly informed me that she sewed for her family and church friends—that's all. That door slammed hard in my face. I went home deeply depressed. *Who needs friends?* I thought. I tried to go to showers and activities that involved church people, but I didn't know where anyone lived, and no one offered to help me find the way. Anger and bitterness are mild words as to how I began to feel. I voiced my concerns to my family, but no one listened.

 Then one really harsh winter I made a crazy decision. I left Rio Vista, my family, and God and went to stay with my cousin in Irving. She lived in a neighborhood where there were lots of children, and I felt connected to the world again. I'm not proud of this, but I couldn't take the isolation anymore. I was twenty-nine, about to turn thirty. Life was passing me by. If I was searching for attention, I sure got it after that. Everyone took notice and began trying to get me to come home. Afterwards, I got a job in Fort Worth at Fort Worth Children's Hospital, and then switched to Boulevard Hospital where Susan worked. My marriage was down the tubes, and my anger toward God was extremely severe. When Wally and I would meet to talk about our future, it always ended in a huge fight. I refused to go back to how things were! Forgiveness appeared impossible.

 I was shocked at how the world looked at things. Everyone I knew expressed to me that if I got a divorce I would get everything—the house, the land, our nice car, and child support. He would get shafted. I didn't really want to hurt Wally like that, yet I felt as if my life had been reduced in a range of monotone colors of flat grays and blacks. Life hit rock bottom.

 Another problem I had to consider. I had left God, but I still talked to Him. I had met some acquaintances at a little bar down the street. I often wondered if Jesus showed up would He take me out of the bar? My spirit was restless, and each time I prayed I would ask God the silliest question. How long can I run from You? Like the prodigal son in Luke 15:11–32, I ran out into the world, but God was waiting for my return. The return was gradual, for there was serious conflict deep inside my heart. Character building happens under the pressure of life. The greatest and strongest trees are those that have weathered many storms. God explains in Isaiah that "those who wait for the Lord will gain new strength; they will mount up with wings like eagles" (Isa. 40:31).

I returned to God as I prayed. I turned it all over to Him and said, "Fix it." I had a blind faith that He would and could fix everything. And once again He was there for me in the most unusual, spectacular manner. I found a poem in a book titled "Shadow of the Almighty" by Elisabeth Elliot that depicts God's character and how He deals with us. He attaches Himself to us, not the other way around.

"We change, He changes not;
"Our Christ can never die.
"His love, not ours, the resting place,
"His truth, not mine, the tie" (p. 158).

If I could wish to be any creature in the world, it would probably be a bird. Imagine flying higher than the tallest snowcapped mountain in the world. Birds have such marvelous lack of restraint as they soar higher and higher. Well, I prayed that God would fix all I'd messed up, and He developed an unbelievably, perfect plan. Wally and I ventured to live together again, but all we did was argue. In hopes of sidetracking our minds, since I was still employed, we decided to look for new furniture. We had always wanted new furniture but couldn't afford it. This would redirect our focus at least temporarily.

Without warning I began to experience things in my body I had never felt before. I thought it was because I was thirty. I approached a nurse one night at work and described my symptoms.

"Sounds like you're pregnant," she answered.

"Well, it can't be that. A really good doctor told me I'd never have a baby," I explained. "That was ruled out a long time ago."

"This may sound strange to you, but your body is always subject to change. You could very well be pregnant."

"Sure, you have a point, but I had the entire tests run, and there's no way possible."

"I've seen stranger things happen. You may be right, but I wouldn't rule it out." She laughed as she continued her duties down the hall.

After my mom listened to some of the symptoms, she suggested I take in a specimen the next morning and let them do a pregnancy test. *Fine, I'll do it*, I thought, *but this is silly. I can't have a baby.*

The following morning I took the specimen to the lab. After about three minutes the lab tech grinned and said, "I hope you have some little baby clothes left. 'Cause you're going to need them."

"Okay, that's enough teasing. You're just saying that. Really? Now don't start like everyone else that I'm going to have a baby. I can't! Besides, that little screwy test can't tell just like that. It takes a doctor to tell you."

"Sharon, we do this test all the time; we're a hospital. And it's 99 percent correct."

I heard her, but nothing was sinking in. I stood and stared. *They don't understand; this can't happen to me. It's not possible*, I thought to myself. Someone led me to a telephone where they called Wally. She handed me the phone, and I told Wally. It sounded like someone else was talking. It didn't seem real that I was saying this. But, no, it was me.

He always had to show off in front of his friends. So he blurted out in a masculine tone, "What in the world have you done now?"

That's all he said to me. I hung up the phone and cried. My

feelings were crushed.

In total contrast to Wally's reaction earlier in the day, when I arrived home and got out of the car I could smell a terrific meal being prepared. I'll never forget the special moment outside Mother's house when I saw Wally bounce out the door, run over to me, grab my things, and hold my hand all the way into the kitchen. He asked me if I was feeling okay. I didn't even know how to respond. *Is this the same man I spoke to this morning?* I thought.

Mother had always been a fantastic cook. She outdid herself that night. But Wally hardly noticed the spread on the table and the smell penetrating the air. He paced back and forth in front of their phone waiting to break the news to his mom. Anticipation filled the air.

If only life were simple. This seemed like the worst time for such a blessed event. Our marriage was in shambles. What was God thinking? Surely this was not the best timing. We were in a crisis, but God knew exactly what He was doing. I just couldn't picture it at the moment.

God hears simple, heartfelt prayers. Prayer is not eloquence, but earnestness. Its definition is not helplessness. It is not a figure of speech, but thoughtfulness and sincerity of the soul. I've never been gifted with the ability to pray eloquent prays, church-approved prayers heard in public. I would be laughed right out of church if my prayers were voiced there. I pray as if God and I are talking over coffee and cake. (No disrespect intended.) Our conversations are nothing more than a very personal friend talking with another friend. Sometimes I use David's writings to praise God by reading Scripture to Him. At other times I raise God high above me to remember my sinful status. But many conversations are just to a faithful Friend.

Prayer in its simplest definition is merely our deepest feelings and desires turned heavenward. As we converse with earthly friends there is often miscommunication. We don't disclose deep, dark secrets of the soul. With God I communicate securely and unthreatened. Even thoughts of suicide do not alarm God. We all want out sometime or another.

What God was doing in my life at that time made no sense to me. But after a long while, I saw everything in my marriage change. My stomach began to grow and expand, and Kerrie and Stevie loved to feel the baby kick. Our entire focus shifted. Wally stopped by every day and spoiled me with a malt, which is the one thing I craved. Being pampered felt incredibly good. We didn't get our new furniture, but we got something so much greater. We grew closer together than ever before.

When this baby decided to come, it was a classic Hollywood experience. I woke up at 2:30 a.m. and yelled, "It's time," with horror and anxiety.

"Are you sure?" he replied sleepily.

"Yes, I'm sure. My water broke and the pains are hard and frequent. Go get mother to watch the kids," I yelled between moans. Susan and John were there, and she told me later I screamed and yelled at Wally lots of things—things I had no idea I said. We drove to the hospital doing eighty to ninety miles per hour. I labored for only three short hours, and then William Mark Stephenson was born at 5:55 a.m.

Elizabeth brought Kerrie and Stevie to the parking lot so I could wave at them. They had never really been away from me. It was so special. Me, the one who couldn't have any children, now had a baby from my own womb. God had blessed me with three. I couldn't take it all in. The next two years we were on the go—two children in elementary school, a baby at home. We still worked on our house and knew that it was like raising children—it would take a lifetime.

Chapter Six

The Author of Our Faith

God is faithful to keep His promises; He alone is our hope (Rom. 15:13). "And we know that God causes all things to work together for good to those who love God, to those who are called according to His purpose" (Rom. 8:28).

A strict belief in fate is the worst kind of slavery, but on the other hand there is comfort in the thought that our prayers move God. For fate is no more than a leaf being tossed to and fro in the wind. But for God's children, He overrules all mutinous accidents and brings them under His laws of fate and makes them all serviceable to His purpose.

The following events are by far the most important and distinct moments of my life. They enabled me to know God better and see His handiworks with 20/20 vision. Have you ever asked the question, "Is there really a God? Does He care about me; does He know I exist? Are my dreams important in the scheme of everything?"

Most people suffer from some sort of blindness. Until things are brought to our attention, we don't see them. They pass right over our heads. My eyes were about to be opened in these next life experiences.

As I reflect, my life was like a puzzle and each piece fell into place just where it should. God became more comprehensible, and I caught a glimpse of His majesty. Every detail fashioned by

His hands. God, who is older than time and greater than death, was manipulating one of His greatest plans while I walked in my earthly tent. Gone was the pomp and spectacle of religion. The fog of theology dissipated. The curtain was momentarily pulled aside so those present could share in its celestial light. "My prayer for this book—without apologies—is that the Surgeon who gives sight to the blind will restore sight to those who are spiritually blind. I pray that Jesus will emerge from a shadowy, unfamiliar, figure out of the fog, and will become a knowable, tangible, touchable, figure that will light your path" (Max Lucado, *God Came Near*, pp. 15–17).

When Thomas saw Jesus after the resurrection, he proclaimed, "My Lord and my God!" Thomas had been a companion, friend, and disciple to Jesus, but only at the end did he really realize who Jesus truly was. He walked, ate, and befriended the Truth for years, but he was blind the whole time. Spiritual blindness can be dangerous if it follows one to eternity.

Working on our huge two-story house got old day after day. But this was Wally's dream, and he was so excited. He enjoyed his land, loved his large family, and was beginning to settle down in life.

One gorgeous spring day Susan and John came to visit the Rio Vista clan. John and Wally headed out to our barn, which Wally had been working on for several months. Mother, Susan, and I were in Mom's kitchen talking over coffee when I happened to gaze out the window and see John and Wally hurrying to John's car. John's shirt was draped over Wally's arm as Wally limped to the car. An alarm went off in my brain. Something happened! I ran to see just as John was pulling away from the driveway.

"What happened?" I yelled.

"Get back, we've got to go!" John screamed back as he flew out of the driveway, squealing his tires. I watched in confusion. Something bad had happened, but there was no clue. Soon we were all standing outside scratching our heads. Daddy and I promptly walked out toward the barn to make sense of it all. We spoke of possibilities, a snake bite perhaps. But upon arrival it took only one glance to locate the blood on the ground and on Wally's power saw. Other than this evidence, we were at a loss as to how badly Wally may have been hurt. Again we all discussed that this could only happen to him. It was always as if someone was out to get him. We gathered around the telephone waiting for news.

Wally had so many physical problems. He lived with a chronic infection that caused his feet to break open and bleed. There was always some kind of treatment going on for this. We burned his socks every month and bought new ones. He fought it constantly. I watched him many mornings grimace as he placed his feet into his boots to go to work. He never knew, but I would cry myself back to sleep wishing his pain would go away. But he never complained.

Finally, the phone rang and Wally was laughing about this new adventure. He almost cut his right index finger completely off. It was barely hanging on by skin. They were going to transport him to a specialist in Fort Worth for surgery. I gathered clothes for him and hurried to the hospital. He was showing off for all the nurses when I arrived. Now he had another story to tell when there was a crowd that would listen.

How odd, but fortunate that John was right there with him. John was a paramedic. God always got Wally through his antics with a certain amount of ease and safety. No matter what happened to him, he always thought it was a fun story to tell later.

Amazingly, life has a way of taking something rather insignificant and turning it into a major turning point. He worked for the T&P Railroad as an electrician and was being placed on a long leave of absence that would last most of the rest of the year. I prayed for Wally, and it seemed God always took care of him. Someone put it like this: "Without God man cannot; without man God will not." My confidence in God's providential care over Wally may seem foolish to some, but the Bible says, *"God's foolishness is wiser than man's wisdom."* Our faith is earnestly important to God. In Hebrews 11, the faith chapter, it indicates we please God if we have faith. "And without faith it is impossible to please Him, for he who comes to God must believe that He is and that He is a rewarder of those who seek Him" (Heb. 11:6).

Several years before we moved to Rio Vista, I had attended a revival at my local church in Arlington, Texas. I recalled the evangelist extending an invitation to all the women present to come the following Monday morning to find out God's prescription in the Bible for saving their husbands. He claimed God had revealed to him that there were many women in the congregation that were concerned for lost husbands. He was correct. About eighty women took advantage of his summons. It scares me now to realize how ignorant of the Bible most of us Christians are, and sermons today are anything but deep.

I can't believe what happened, and I'll never be convinced it was of God. Many women were very concerned for their loved ones, but this is what happened. The meeting began, and to our surprise, he began to explain that God had led him in another direction. He explained that if we were concerned for our husband we needed to buy a certain book and read it. He completely changed the subject, and I've no idea what he said. I left there that day frustrated, angry, and about to blow my top. Surely, he knew why all those women had come. I walked through my door at home, threw my books on the couch, and screamed. *I try to do what is right and this is what I get!* I thought.

I know now we cannot depend on human beings. Preachers are not God, and they make mistakes. But to the world, they represent God. How many ladies went home that day and lost all faith because of this incident. Nonetheless, God knew the leap of faith we all took by simply being there. We didn't get our information, but God always honors faith. He sees your hurting heart if you are concerned for someone else's salvation. In the following events, you will understand that He blesses even your hurting heart. You will be surprised.

I won't apologize for loving Wally and wanting to spend eternity with him. God places burdens on our hearts, and we can't change it. I'm amazed when a missionary says God laid it upon their heart to go around the world to tell others about Jesus. But I figure God places a burden on every saved heart. His love spews out and overflows in our lives because of our burdens. Without the burden there's no prayer; without prayer there's no response; without a response there's no change.

Early one morning as the sun was about to emerge and a small speck of light peeked through the darkness of the night, I had a dream. Wally was already up plowing with my father's old tractor he had purchased so us city folks could be real farmers. He was making his rounds around our thirty acres alone in the pasture; he appeared so content. In that moment of silence, I noticed these lovely, white birds swarming all around him. They landed on him, and he had to brush them away. Then they dove into the freshly tilled earth. I had never seen him look so fulfilled. My dream lasted only seconds, but I imagined Wally in heaven working for God, and it brought instant gratification to my mind and my heart.

Well, we all have our little eccentric ways. Everyone knows mine. Even if I'm visiting and someone leaves a light on in an empty room, I turn the light off. It drives me crazy. At night my daddy used to watch the stars on their back porch, then make the long walk through their kitchen and on into the living room where mother watched television and read a book each evening. Thus the kitchen light stayed on all evening unless I showed up.

"Mother, the kitchen light is off, Sharon must be here," he frequently said in a teasing manner.

"But, Sharon, why do you turn our lights off when you don't even have to pay our electric bill?"

"You know what, daddy? The electric company should give me an award the way I save for them. Just call it habit or something.

I don't know why I do it. I'm kin to you and look at all the crazy things you do to save. Let's just leave it at that, shall we?" My father didn't stop to think the acorn didn't fall far from the tree. We went back and forth about the subject, but it was true. He was as tight as they come, and I'm sure I got it from him.

The reason for that short story is to demonstrate that Wally knew me pretty well himself. So, normally our conversation before he left for work was almost always about the porch light. "I'm gone; turn the porch light off in a few minutes," he would yell.

"Okay, see you later. I'll turn it off as soon as you're gone," I would normally yell back.

At last we had plenty of time to work on the house, but there wasn't as much money. One day Wally gathered the kids around the table as we had coffee.

"I've exhausted all my ideas—my mind is at a standstill. How can we afford to work on this house?" he stated. "Hey, what about you guys? How would you like to help us? There's a way," he asked the kids who were wide eyed by now. "Okay, for starters, would you let us borrow the money you've saved in your piggy banks to buy some paneling, and I'll repay you when I go back to work?"

"Yes!" they screamed as they jumped around, excited to be of help to us.

"Okay, for starters," Wally replied, "run and get your piggy banks you got for Christmas, and we'll see how full they are." Fortunately for us, grandparents had poked some dollar bills in each one. They all ran eagerly to their rooms to find their lost or forgotten piggy banks. They probably uncovered them from toy boxes or under the beds. They had saved enough money that when we mingled our own with theirs it pretty much covered the paneling for the whole den. Most of the progress on our home had been slow, but now we made great strides.

God did a real work on me during these months; He changed me in many ways. The bond between Wally and I was mushrooming. Before I realized it, I became the kind of wife I should have always been.

One morning as he was on the phone with a lumber company about supplies, I brought him over a cup of coffee and set it beside him. I'll always remember the look on his face. For a second we both knew we were different. It was one of those moments one really can't explain. It just happened. Our home was peaceful and comfortable. What I had yearned for in our marriage, I finally possessed. The following story explains what I experienced.

"When I was a little boy, my mother used to embroider a great deal. I would sit at her knee and look up from the floor and ask what she was doing. She informed me she was embroidering. I told her it looked like a mess from where I was. As from the other side I watched her work within the boundaries of the little round hoop that she held in her hand. I complained to her that it sure looked messy from where I sat. She would smile at me, look down and gently say, 'My son, you go about your playing for a while, and when I am finished with my embroidering, I will put you on my knee and let you see it from my side.' I would wonder why she was using some dark threads along with the bright ones and why they seemed so jumbled from my view. A few minutes would pass and then I would hear Mother's voice say, 'Son, come and sit on my knee.' This I did only to be surprised and thrilled to see a beautiful flower or a sunset. I could not believe it, because from underneath it looked so messy.

"Then Mother would say to me, 'My son, from underneath it did look messy and jumbled, but you did not realize that there was a pre-drawn plan on the top. It was a design. I was only following it. Now look at it from my side and you will see what I was doing.'

"Many times through the years I have looked up to my heavenly Father and said, 'Father, what are You doing?' He has answered, 'I am embroidering your life.' I say, 'But it looks like a mess to me. It seems so jumbled. The threads seem so dark.

Why can't they all be bright?' The Father seems to tell me, 'My child, you go about your business of doing My business, and one day I will bring you to Heaven and put you on My knee and you will see the plan from My side'" (Author Unknown, *God's Embroidery*).

This is me at 17 years old, at my last recital.

The Author of Our Faith 67

This is a picture of Wally's team at General Dynamics were he worked on the F-111.

This is a picture of our wedding. June 15, 1962.

This is the night of Kerrie's first piano recital. She was very nervous.

This picture was taken one month before Wally died.

This was Wally working on our house in Rio Vista. We knew it would take a life time but he enjoyed every minute.

Sharon Wilkerson's second grade class (2002)

This is a picture of my son, Mark & his son, Avery visiting Wally's grave.

Mark never knew his father, Wally. Mark was only 2 years old when his father died.

Chapter Seven

"I Am"

While on this earth, Jesus declared that He was one with God. The title "I Am" expresses God's dependability, love, and faithfulness in every way, even in the smallest details of our lives, as you will experience with me (John 8:38–58).

Sometimes as I sit at a funeral, I have this strange sensation that the lucky one is the one lying down at the front. Their battle is finished. There is so much pain and sorrow in this world that at times it's hard to go on. Trusting our eternity to God and His plan for us is really not natural. It is not of this world; it is a blind trust. Without a doubt it goes against the grain. But in Hebrews 11:32, the writer explains that he hasn't time to tell about all those in the past who walked completely by faith, for there's way too many to speak of. They simply trusted in God. My testimony is living proof the He rewards those who endeavor to find Him.

"By faith Enoch was taken up so that he should not see death ... he was pleasing to God. And without faith it is impossible to please Him, for he who comes to God must believe that He is" (Heb. 11:5, 6).

In the late 1970s the kids and I used to watch *All in the Family*, a situation comedy on television adored my many. The main character, Archie Bunker, on many occasions gave his comical rendition and conclusion of various biblical truths. On one segment he explained his interpretation of faith. I don't know that I remember it word for word, but I'll say it how my memory serves me. When badgered by his son-in-law, the meathead who is a confirmed atheist, Archie attempted to make clear his interpretation of what faith means. His explanation of faith is that it is something people believe in that no one in their right mind would believe in! His perception of biblical truths was always amusing, yet perhaps we can glean some truth out of this preposterous declaration. The Bible says that the cross to those who are trusting in it is everything to them, but to those who do not believe, it is foolishness.

"For the word of the cross is foolishness to those who are perishing, but to us who are being saved it is the power of God.... Because the foolishness of God is wiser than men, and the weakness of God is stronger than men" (1 Cor. 1:18, 25).

Sometimes hesitantly but obediently we jump out there and emphatically trust God's plan. Then He proves we can trust Him when He acts upon our needs and desires.

The Stephenson family was allowed some special months for a purpose. It's important for me to remember every detail concerning the next two months, January and February of 1977. Sometime in mid-January Wally came home on a gorgeous, warm sunny day with a motorcycle in the back of his truck. It had been a warm winter in Texas. Mother and I peered out her kitchen window in shock and disbelief. We all hated motorcycles.

"What has he gone and done now?" Mother asked in frustration. "Doesn't he realize he's accident prone?"

"Yeah, and you know what? He'll be the one dead; I'll just be a widow," I stated, giving it little thought. I hurried to our driveway where he and John were deep in discussion about how to unload it from the truck. Wally's enthusiastic spirit is so animated it's hard to be depressed. He was quite excited with his new toy. But I had so many reservations. I told him what I'd said to mother, but he barely noticed. They unloaded it and conversations about the danger of motorcycles surfaced, but this didn't deter Wally one bit. When the kids saw daddy's new addition, they all demanded that he take them for a ride. My heart cringed. He explained to them that he needed to learn how to ride it first. Oh, that made me feel a lot better. But then he said that some man he worked with had ridden one for twenty years and was going to teach Wally how to jump curbs. I thought I would die.

After a couple of weeks, the kids heard him say he was going to ride it to work, and it was strange because they seemed to sense the danger.

"Daddy, *please* don't ride it yet. We don't want you to get hurt," they all said. I grabbed him and hugged him real tight.

"You know we're right. It's too soon," I added. Kerrie even had tears in her eyes. Finally, he dismissed the idea. We hugged that day for a long time. Our last hug. I didn't realize how special that moment was. But winning that argument didn't mean it was over. He eventually began to drive it to work, and I continued to pray for him.

One night about 10:00 p.m. I was in the middle of our nightly ritual of getting three little monkeys ready for bed when Wally got ready to leave for work.

"Get your pajamas on, teeth brushed. Please leave her alone; ya'll stop fighting. And will you quit jumping on the bed," I yelled as the routine progressed. There was always a process in settling them down before lights out. Knowing well these night raids, I normally only had enough time to yell at Wally, "Goodbye or see you tomorrow," or "Okay dear, I'll flip the porch light off when you're gone."

Amazingly over all the noise in the house, I heard the loud roar of the bike as he raced the motor. I pulled back the curtains just in time to see his small taillights on the back of his motorcycle before he turned onto the main road in front of our house. A wave of distress filled my heart as it raced, and my imagination anchored in nightmarish images. With a grimace, fear filled my being. It appeared to be a normal evening, but not for me. Up close the bike looked so big, but now in the dark on a country road it appeared really small. He made the turn toward major highways and traffic, and suddenly I felt horrible and sick—my emotions took a nosedive. The realization of our need for him inundated me. *We can't lose him—he's way too important to us all.* Brief flashes of what could happen appeared in my mind and then disappeared. I needed to be strong, but my fears intensified despite what I wanted.

Throughout our lives, as weird as it seems, memories are forever etched in our minds. I still see him with the two little lights on the back going out into a big world on something so small. I decided to pray—night raids or not.

"God, please take care of our daddy, because we love him and need him so much, in Jesus name, Amen." I voiced this prayer quietly while staring at my sweetheart taking off into the dark night. God placed a song in my mind as soon as I prayed. He's always there to comfort. The song is "Tis So Sweet To Trust In Jesus." Our hindsight is 20/20—God's foreknowledge is 20/20. I relaxed.

The subsequent weeks were anything but unforgettable. For February the weather was unbelievably warm and beautiful. Wally got in plenty of practice time on the bike.

Stevie had recently acquired a new friend at school, and one weekend he begged me to let him spend the night. I agreed, so we drove a long distance into the country, located his house, and I met his mom. After we talked a while, she was in favor of their sleepover. So he packed his overnight clothes, and I reminded him to pack some clothes for church. On the way home, he voiced his opinion about church, and it startled me.

"Mrs. Stephenson, I really don't want to go to church with ya'll," he said in a small, timid voice. "The devil is at church. I know cause that's all our preacher ever talks about. Do I have to go, cause I'm really scared?"

He wouldn't let it rest. "Couldn't Stevie skip just this one time? I'm afraid of the devil; our preacher makes him sound evil. I don't want to go, please." He had tears in his eyes. Little children—you never know how they will perceive abstract things.

I thought before speaking, something I wish I did more of. "You know what? God is at our church, and the Bible tells us that God is love. We don't talk about the devil. We talk about God's love," I assured him. I felt so sorry for him—this small five-year-old boy voicing these peculiar concerns. I explained that he had nothing to fear unless I sang a solo. Stevie chuckled, for he had heard my singing before. Boy did he agree!

After the worship service the following morning, Ronnie Lyles, our pastor, came over to greet me and say hello. We entered into a conversation, and I explained what this little boy had said the day before. Ronnie agreed that many churches talk more about the devil than the love of God. That's what they zero in on. Children don't understand because they don't think abstractly like adults.

"You know, Sharon, a lot of preachers focus more on hell than on heaven. It can scare children. They don't see both sides, so their vision is limited. But, one last thought before I go home to eat—everyone is afraid of what they don't understand." He was speaking as he made his way to the back of the church.

"Yeah, like death," I said without realizing it didn't fit in with our conversation. No one had mentioned death. But it just rolled off my tongue. For a second there, it was as if someone else had said it. I was hoping Ronnie hadn't heard me—and as fast as he retreated out the back door, I don't think he did. I felt a little embarrassed. As I stated it I had an uncanny sensation that engulfed my emotions—only for a second. Why had I said it? Oh well, I got my things together and gathered the kids so we could go home and get some lunch. I dismissed it out of my mind.

A feeling is defined in Webster's Dictionary as "to be conscious of an inward impression, state of mind, to be aware of, to believe or think or experience." No words can adequately express how I would feel inside about many things that were soon to be fashioned in my consciousness during the next week. Ronnie and I were having a casual conversation, which we'd done many times before, and what I said didn't fit in at all. It caused me to reflect for a second or two. But I dismissed it as a silly quirk.

Strange occurrences and thoughts happened throughout the week. Yet, for some reason each time I paused and meditated on the idea for a few seconds, allowing it to mull over in my mind, I would simply dismiss it and go on. But each incident in time would come back to me and become extremely significant. I was a busy housewife raising three rowdy kids; I couldn't think about any one subject for very long.

On Wednesday, February 16, I worked hard cleaning house so we could visit Susan and John that afternoon at their home in Fort Worth. There was laundry to do, so I began there. As I rummaged through the pockets of Wally's jeans I found more gadgets and junk. If I'd washed all of it, it would have been more than the clothes.

While emptying the pockets of his work clothes, I had the most overwhelming sensation hit me like a brick. Talk about a feeling. I had never felt this way before, ever! My memory was in a fog—reality seemed to come in pieces. It was a delight and joy to be busy doing what I enjoyed—taking care of my family. But vaguely I began to think about a word. The word was premonition. I'd never had a premonition. I almost didn't know if it was real or a hallucination, conjured up by collisions of wayward neurons in my brain. That word rolled around in my head and I couldn't shake it. *I should have control over what I think*, I told myself.

Eventually, like it or not, I went in search of Mark. He was two and could be hurt. Well, Mark wasn't hurt, but he had baptized the bike with some red transmission fluid Wally had sitting just within his reach. Mark and I marched to the barn where Wally was working, and I demanded he put things up high so Mark could not reach them. I also informed him his bike would need a good cleaning. I didn't tell Wally about my outlandish, uneasy feeling that had overpowered me. As strange as the sensation had been, in all simplicity I thought to myself, I was glad Mark was okay. I dismissed it.

Late in the afternoon, we left for Fort Worth to visit Susan and John who had finally become parents. Susan's baby girl,

Ingrid, was only a few weeks old. We were all excited because she too had waited a long time for motherhood. Wally rode the motorcycle, and we followed close behind. He would have to leave for work from their house. The kids really had fun watching their father ride it. Mark wasn't two yet, and his language was so cute to listen to.

"I see my daddy on dat big bike. Look, Mommy, dares our daddy wit a big red helmet on his head. Catch up wit him, Mommy, catch up wit him. You dwive to slow," Mark shouted out with joy.

"Yeah, Mom," the others chimed in. "You're going to slow. We keep losing him. Drive faster," they yelled.

"Okay, okay, guys. But there are other people on the road, and I have to watch out for them. I'll go as fast as I can, but maybe your dad needs to slow down a little." Somehow in traffic we eventually lost sight of Wally, but as I turned the corner onto Susan's street, we saw that Wally had already arrived. He was parked in the yard and was energetically embellishing in deep conversation about his new story of how a lady cut him off and he had had to jump a curb as he made his way there. I flinched as I walked by and had no choice but to hear the new, scary story about him and his bike ride. I was not too happy.

We all made our way to the nursery. Ingrid was sound asleep, but oh so pretty. After much conversation about babies and bikes, Wally decided to take his family out to eat before he had to leave for work. This was rare, and since I stayed at home all the time, it sounded like quite a treat. He located a small place that sold hamburgers. We were forced to eat in the car, which resulted in French fries and catsup everywhere. *This was a queer situation*, I thought. *He's brave enough to ride a motorcycle, but not brave enough to take three children out to a nice restaurant.*

As we munched down hamburgers and fries in our lovely, but cramped conditions, Wally began to reminisce about how we wrote letters to each other when he was in the navy. There was this 1960s song that he always quoted. It was called "You're

Sixteen, You're Beautiful, and You're Mine." He always left the "You're Beautiful" part out as I reminded him. Our conversation became nostalgic before we realized it, and we teased each other back and forth.

"What's up with that?" I asked.

"Well, maybe I meant to leave it out. I'll never tell," he joked. Eating with the kids in the car didn't surprise me, but talking about our dating years was far from normal. Wally didn't live his life looking back—always forward. He was never overly romantic. This conversation was definitely out of the ordinary. But then, women are romantic, and I enjoyed the moment for what it was.

Late in the evening at Susan's house, I told Mother about the incident earlier in the day. She and Daddy were staying at Susan's to help her with the baby. I told her of the overpowering, foreboding sensation that had engulfed me as I was going through Wally's jeans emptying his pockets before washing them. Never had I ever felt such a strong emotion before, and it's still fresh on my mind. I shared my feelings with her and asked her opinion concerning my thoughts. I explained that no matter what I couldn't shake the feeling at the time. While digging through his pockets, I merely dropped the pants on the floor and said out loud "premonition."

"Why can't I get that word out of my head?" I asked. There was no clear-cut answer. But the emotion had been so intense, I couldn't help but ask why it had occurred in the first place when nothing like that had ever happened to me before. Stevie and Kerrie had been in troubling situations before, yet nothing like that had ever happened. I just couldn't make sense of my feelings and fears.

The following day was Thursday, February 17. The same 'ole' monotonous routine was before me—kids to feed, a house to clean, and piles of laundry to wash. Even Wally's near death accident was not out of the ordinary. He ran into the house screaming and yelling at me because he had had an accident in the garage and I didn't respond to his pleas for help. Our garage is where he works on cars, and it is not attached to the house. I hadn't heard a thing, and he was mad. He'd been working on a truck for weeks, and today the pick-up truck that was behind the one he was working on lost its brakes and plowed directly into the one he was working on causing it to lunge forward. He was standing in front of the truck but managed to jump onto a very high shelf, which saved him from harm, but he was pinned in-between the truck and the shelf screaming for help. Fortunately, our neighbor happened to be walking his fence line when she heard Wally. He stormed into the house quite upset with me for not hearing him.

"I could've been crushed and died out there, and you would've never even known it. How could you not hear me?" he snapped.

"How can you say that?" I screamed in my defense. "If I'd heard you, I would have come running, and you know it!" My feathers were quickly ruffled, but I backtracked. "I'm sorry I didn't hear you, but I honestly heard nothing. This house is pretty noisy in here with three kids and the television blaring. I'm sorry. I'm glad you're okay."

"Whatever, I could've been killed and none of ya'll would've even known it." He walked away, continuing to mumble other things as his voice trailed off to nothing. He headed back to the garage. Soon our anger subsided and the rest of the day was uneventful. We were both *way* too busy to argue much.

While Kerrie was at school, Stevie watched cartoons and Mark took a nap. I finally sat down at the dining room table in the afternoon while it was quiet and read a small piece or two from the *Reader's Digest*. I always enjoyed the short articles because I could get to the end quickly as opposed to a long book. I had a difficult time sitting for very long, so this magazine was perfect for me. Each month the first story I'd read was "Drama in Real Life." I enjoyed the true stories, for they held my interest best.

This month's article was about a little girl who fell onto a subway track in the New York City subway station as she and her mom waited for a train. "It was a moment frozen in time …" is how the article began. I might as well have been right there. I sensed the author's anxiety. I hurriedly scanned the pages, thoroughly engrossed in the story. The author wrote about a true event in an atypical style. As each incident occurred, he explained that only a few seconds had passed. As the scenes unfolded, I became completely out of breath. I know I laid the magazine aside a few times while reading so I could breathe again and get my bearings. I was really into this.

The scene took place in a busy subway station where a large crowd of people stood on a platform awaiting a train. Suddenly and without warning they were all stunned beyond belief. A small girl accidentally fell onto the tracks below. A certain young man just coming up the stairs from beneath the platform was approaching the area. He quickly noticed what had happened, and as he observed the scene, his eyes fixed upon the ghastly horror before them. He scanned the crowd and realized no one knew what to do. Everyone stood there helplessly looking on. His mind began to race for a solution, but he knew whoever endeavored to save her would probably be killed as a train thundered toward the area where her body lay limp and motionless. He was positive there was no time to lose.

If I try to help her, there's a good possibility I'll die also, but how can I just stand here like the others and do nothing? he asked himself.

The response time was limited for sure. *If I help, then two people will die a senseless death.* But it was for certain she would die without intervention. For some bizarre reason, he felt compelled to jump onto the tracks, even though the train was merely seconds away. Hopefully by some sheer miracle he would save the girl.

The author spoke of each incident as if it were taking place in just a matter of seconds— each thought, action, and heartbeat. I was on the edge of my seat as I continued to read. My pulse raced as I became a part of each scene.

Everyone could feel the train coming quickly as it barreled down the track at thirty miles per hour toward the small, crumpled body lying on the tracks. Feeling more and more compelled to do something, the young man jumped into the deep well in a feeble attempt to save her. Now on the tracks he could feel the heavy, metal train and see its lights as it thundered toward where he and the girl were now both at the mercy of time. If he didn't think and act with quick precision, both would die in only seconds.

The author continued using the term fifteen seconds, ten seconds, five seconds, as each sequence of events happened and each thought entered into the man's mind. He quickly reached the little girl, so tiny and helpless, lifted her up, and with all his power managed to throw her limp body onto the platform above, knocking over a number of spectators.

Now it was his turn. Would he make it in time? The train was almost there. The headlights blinded him, and he estimated he had approximately five seconds or less. He desperately tried several unsuccessful attempts to throw his body onto the platform above. Suddenly many arms were reaching out to grab him. He grabbed hold of them, and they pulled him up and out just as the train went by. In his mind, he knew he would probably lose his legs. When he was safe, he looked down and discovered to his surprise that he had lost only part of the edge of his right shoe. The little girl was saved, and he was fine also. The article stated that he received a special citizen's award for heroism from New York City (Warren R. Young, *Reader's Digest*, "There's a Girl On The Tracks," February 1977, pp. 91–95).

I slapped the magazine down on the table, almost knocking over my coffee. Shaken by what had been revealed in this article in an overbearing manner, my breathing had become quick and shallow. What a story!

When Kerrie bounced into the house from school, she began to whine and whimper that she was in dire need of crayons at school. Her complaint was that someone was stealing hers. I ignored her as long as possible, for I knew this was way too trivial for her dad to want to make a long trip to Cleburne just to buy crayons.

"Daddy, can we go to the store and get crayons. Mine keep getting stolen, and I'm supposed to have them every day—teacher says," Kerrie whined again.

"You know what? That sounds like a good idea. While we're there, we'll stop and get ice cream from Ashburn's."

"Oh, yay! Yay!" the kids screamed as they jumped around. All were delighted.

"Everyone off to the car. Hurry. I've got lots to do when we get back," Wally said as we all grabbed ours coats and things and raced to the car. For some reason, only I seemed to realize this was out of the ordinary. My husband, who was also my friend, was changing right before my eyes. He was quite the family man now. I had longed and hoped for this for years, and after all, hope is a waking dream.

It took us twenty minutes to get to Cleburne. On our way I shared the *Reader's Digest* article with Wally in a tone of excitement and exhilaration. Wally was attentive, a real active listener. Even his body language revealed to me he was interested.

When we arrived at the five and dime store, we purchased Kerrie's school supplies and made our way to Ashburn's. The kids raced on in even before we could get our hands on the car door to open them. Wally and I remained in the car for a few moments, and I continued to bend his ears. There was this test they always have in the reader you can take to determine if you have a high IQ. Just for fun I had taken the test and was rated a genius. I had quite a laugh over that. Wally knew about my inferiority complex. But it was still odd what he did. He grabbed my hand and began to expose his true feelings.

"Sharon, you're always thinking you can't go to college or can't do what you'd like because you're too dumb. I've been married to you for fifteen years now, and I know if you make up your mind to do something, you'll do it. I have total faith in your abilities—and that's the truth!" He not only held my hand, but he gazed into my eyes a little longer than usual. I knew he loved me, but he didn't seem quite like himself.

My greatest desire had been to go straight into college after high school. But I'd fallen in love with a man in the navy. Since I hadn't felt I'd be successful in college, I chose marriage. But I loved him and desperately wanted to be with him. I had placed my other dream on hold.

Unusual events continued to take place, but I didn't care. Life was good. I was happy, and all could remain this way forever as far as I was concerned. The evening was uneventful and ended normal. Wally left for work around 10:00 p.m., and I tangled with the kids through the nightly routine until finally they were quiet and in bed.

Turn the page in a novel and you never know what you'll get. Will someone get married? Will someone die? It's all a mystery. And we all enjoy a good mystery. But life is like that sometimes. A new day dawns, and what will it bring? Joy, sorrow, boredom—who knows? *We* don't know, that's for certain. There are uncertainties that slice the routine right in half—knock it down and cause explosions all around. Comfortable—that's what we want. Nothing moving, nothing changing. We take life for granted, and without worry or thought we just know it will continue on forever until we are stunned into the realization that anything can change it—and change it forever. One tiny incident.

Well, without asking our advice, the sun came up and Friday, February 18, 1977, dawned bright and beautiful. Kerrie and Stevie raced to the big yellow school bus in front of the house. I busied myself making breakfast for Wally and Mark. Wally and I lingered a while after coffee, making plans for the day. Just as he headed upstairs to go to bed, our neighbor stopped by and consulted with him about buying a planter to attach to my father's tractor. Sleep now was the last thing on Wally's mind. He wanted that planter. So off they went to the bank.

Before I knew it, lunch was upon us, and since Stevie got

home at noon, we decided to have a picnic. It was a gorgeous day for February—we had to take advantage of the springlike weather. Nature was fooled and trees were budding. After lunch the boys and I walked down to the creek and back. We saw Wally with our neighbor driving back and forth along the road, and they yelled and waved. I knew he needed to sleep before work that night, and I began to get a little worried.

Later in the afternoon my emotions took a nosedive. For no apparent reason, I became disheartened, gloomy, and forlorn. I dismissed it as merely a bad mood. I reminded myself that everyone gets a little depressed from time to time. No big deal! Perhaps I was concerned about Wally's rest—I really didn't know.

John, my brother-in-law, came to visit at around 3:00 p.m. and brought us great news. He and Susan, along with their new baby, were moving down to their land near us. We were all elated. Now there would be Wally and me and our kids, my mother and father, and John and Susan and Ingrid. We would all live close, and none of us would be lonely. I thought that with all this great news perhaps my depression would dissipate.

Wally's newly purchased planter arrived late in the afternoon, and he tried it out on our thirty acres. We were beginning to feel like real farmers. The kids played along the sidelines, watching their dad while they tumbled and played. It had turned out to be a great day. We'd been working daily on our home and making great strides. Everything was coming together. Life couldn't get better than this.

So what was wrong with me? I wanted to slap myself. As evening drew near, my heart again for no reason became dismal—my mood melancholy. I anxiously ventured to shake off this unwanted mindset, but to no avail. Alluded to earlier in the book, Webster describes feelings as a state of mind. No where in the definition does it indicate that it will make sense. At this moment, it made no sense at all.

While questioning this attack on my emotions, I desperately tried to think of answers. Was I worried about Wally? After all, he hadn't had any sleep all day. As for circumstances and weather, both were incredibly perfect. One thing I knew as a mother and wife, I had plenty to do. Supper had to be cooked, so I busied myself to try and take away the depression.

Late in the evening after our company left Wally dragged in with extreme fatigue written all over his face. He headed for our room with instructions to wake him up around 9:30 p.m. That would give him three hours of sleep.

"Do not yell at me or get mad if I yell at you when you wake me up. I don't want to fight tonight. I'm too tired!" he murmured. The bedroom door slammed.

No, we didn't have time to fight tonight. He was never easy to get up and could be quite harsh at times. My sensitive feelers stuck out like little prickly pears. But I knew he was right—get him up, and get out of there sharply. That was my focus.

After he retired upstairs for a short rest, the kids and I began our nightly routine, which they enjoyed immensely. Everyone was involved. We had an extra large living room called our piano fun room. I would play rhythmic songs as they danced around in circles. Mark, our baby, followed his brother and sister's lead. He knocked them down and intentionally tumbled over them as they fell. They laughed hysterically, singing parts of songs, whatever they could remember. It became a routine we all loved and enjoyed.

Tonight as I played the most upbeat music I knew, all their favorites, my heart sunk with an apprehension and dread worse than I'd ever known. My spirit felt paralyzed and dark. It was as if someone or something had laid an exceptionally heavy object on me, and I was slowly sinking down into a pit. I was extremely apprehensive, but about what I didn't know. I kept wiping away tears I couldn't explain. The children just thought my allergies were really bad that night. All this had begun around noon and had progressively worsened as the day wore on. These feelings came out of the blue for no apparent reason. *Maybe I'm going crazy*, I thought at one point. To this day, I cannot describe my feelings accurately. There are no words to adequately describe my inner mindset that day.

Around 9:30 I reluctantly went upstairs to wake Wally. Our usual argument almost erupted, but we both managed to keep our cool. He was grouchy, but nothing escalated between us. As he foresaw, we had no time to argue. I quickly raced down the steps and turned on the evening news. By this time the kids were in bed, and the house was quiet so I could sit peacefully and watch television. As I reflected upon the day, it was not good, and I couldn't understand why.

Wally walked down the stairs, sat down at the dining room table, and began pulling up his boots. We discussed his riding the motorcycle as opposed to driving the truck, but he was determined to ride the bike. I was aware of his lack of sleep, and I worried. We spoke little but our eyes made contact several times. He could always read me.

"Honey, what's wrong with you?" he asked me attentively. "You look depressed or something." Maybe he noticed because I was so quiet, but I hadn't a clue how he sensed my mood so accurately. Normally I would have voiced what I was mad about, but I said nothing. I think that clued him in somewhat. I wasn't talking at all.

After he approached me about the subject, I explained my depression and simply commented that I'd feel better in the morning after a night's sleep. I spoke to him in a monotone voice while staring at the television. He walked across the room where I was curled up in a chair and bent down beside me and gave me a kiss.

"I love you," he said softly.

"I'll just finish watching the news and go to bed early," I replied despondently. "I'm sure I'll feel better in the morning."

None of this scenario was ordinary, but I was trying hard not to think anymore. I was too glum to notice. However, I can't forget the One in control. God works powerfully in our lives much of the time when we are totally oblivious to His presence.

Wally gathered his things together that he needed for work. He grabbed his coat, gloves, and motorcycle helmet preparing to walk out the door. I quietly sat curled up in the chair trying to relax while watching the 10:00 p.m. news. He made his way over to the back door, and then turned and faced me. He stood there with helmet in hand for a few seconds before saying, "I'll see you in the morning, honey,"

That's all. I barely looked up. My eyes perhaps met his for one second, and then returned to the television. "Okay," I acknowledged casually with a sigh. He turned and walked out the door.

Chapter Eight

My Strength

Life is one adjustment after another, and the pathway to victory often goes through a valley of sorrow or suffering. But with God we have an unshakable hope. No matter the degree of suffering. He is present and at work for us (Ps. 91).

God sometimes washes the eyes of His children with tears for He is spoiling us of what otherwise might have spoiled us. When He makes the world too hot for us to hold, we let it go. Oftentimes affliction comes to us to make us sober, not sad. It doesn't come to make us sorry, but wise. It doesn't come to impoverish us, but to enrich us, as the plow enriches the field. It comes to multiply our joy, as the planted seed multiplied a thousandfold.

From the instant I glanced up at Wally and he turned and walked out the door was probably two or three seconds of my lifetime. Down through the years it has become a moment frozen in time for me. How significant those few seconds were, yet neither of us could possibly have known. It's not a human thing to know the future. Thoughts, sensations, and understanding all would come later concerning this incredibly special moment. I recall so clearly the details of each of the following events, and my deepest prayer is that I can and will describe them as accurately as is humanly possible. God was involved and responsible for every detail. The following events changed my life and my faith in Him forever.

We are not always responsible for the situations we encounter in life, but we are accountable for the manner in which we react to them. God orchestrated the subsequent events and was there to see to it that the job was fulfilled in a perfect, timely manner. In fact, His timing was precise, and He had everything under control. He demonstrated perfect love and without it all would have been loss. My mind cannot and will not fathom this ordeal without His amorous, compassionate presence through it all. He was no longer walking alongside of me—He was carrying me!

"One night a man had a dream. He dreamed he was walking along the beach with the Lord. Across the sky flashed scenes from his life. For each scene, he noticed two sets of footprints in the sand; one belonging to him, and the other to the Lord.

"When the last scene of his life flashed before him, he looked back at the footprints in the sand. He noticed that many times along the path of life there was only one set of footprints. He also noticed that it happened at the very lowest and saddest times in his life. This really bothered him, and he questioned the Lord about it.

"'Lord, you said that once I decided to follow You, You'd walk with me all the way. But I noticed that during the most troublesome times in my life, there is only one set of footprints. I don't understand why when I needed You most You would leave me.'

"The Lord replied, 'My son, my precious child, I love you and would never leave you. During your times of trial and suffering, when you see only one set of footprints, it was then that I carried you'" (Author Unknown, "Footprints").

The news ended around 10:30 p.m., and I went straight to bed only to be startled by the telephone ringing a short time later. I jumped out of bed to answer it thinking it must be the middle of the night. *Who could be calling?* I contemplated. I must have fallen right to sleep because it was only 11:20 p.m. A stranger on the other end of the line began asking me questions. I could barely think since I was still half asleep.

"Would you have known someone who would've been traveling through Burleson around 10:50 riding a motorcycle?" a lady asked me.

"Yes, my husband would've been traveling that way," I replied nervously. At this point I was still not fully awake. "He would have gone through Burleson close to that time on a motorcycle on his way to work. Why?" I asked.

There was a long pause that seemed an eternity as she groped for the right words. She explained there had been a wreck.

"I want you to know I prayed with him while holding his hand after the accident. What you need to do now is call the Burleson Police Department, and they can tell you where the ambulance has taken him."

"Yes, yes, I'll do it right away," I fearfully answered. That's all I remember of our conversation. My mind began racing even before we finished talking. Questions bombarded me. Who was this person who had called me? Surely there's no connection to me. It was certainly a mistake. But my mind told me differently. How was I even functioning now? Only God knew. It was as if I was on autopilot. I moved, spoke, and breathed as if I were in someone else's body. I grabbed the phone book on the table beside the phone and my fingers, shaking visibly, scanned the pages in search for the Burleson Police Station. I found it and dialed the number.

"Yes," an officer informed me, "there was a motorcycle accident on Highway 174. The young man was taken by ambulance to John Peter Smith Hospital in Fort Worth."

Instantaneously, I telephoned Susan's house where Mother and Daddy were still staying. I quickly informed them of the strange call I'd received and explained what the police had told me. Fear gripped my heart, body, and soul. I urged them to call Wally's mom, Elizabeth, who lived in Arlington to inform her, and I pleaded with them to all meet me there. Suddenly it hit me like a slap in the face. I was all alone. My only neighbors were even gone. How was I to meet them? How would I get to the hospital? I couldn't leave the kids home alone.

My church—my mind raced as I thought of who lived close to me. Without thought I called my preacher—something I never do. Their lives are so busy, and it was late.

"Sure, we'll be right over. Give us a minute. We just walked in the door from a trip to Fort Worth," Brenda, our pastor's wife, informed me. By the time they arrived, I was trembling and way too upset to drive. Ronnie offered to drive me while Brenda placed their sleepy son on my sofa and stayed to watch the kids. On the drive there Ronnie ventured to calm me down. Anxiety streamed from every pore. I couldn't hide it.

"Sharon, do you know if the police called it a one-vehicle accident?"

"No, I don't remember them using those words at all, and I didn't think to ask."

"What I'm trying to explain. It could be something so simple. He could have hit a pole, fell into a ditch, hit a parked car, or something minor. You may be getting upset over nothing. I'm sure when we get to the hospital, you'll find out that he's fine."

I promptly realized Ronnie thought the situation was not grave. But I knew Wally. Whenever he was in any kind of accident, he *always* called me after the fact. And since we'd been married, he'd had numerous accidents. The most recent accident was when he'd cut his finger off, and he had called me from the emergency room to inform me everything was okay. I knew his ways, and I hadn't received a call from him. Besides the lady had stated she held his hand and prayed with him. Certain facts told me the situation was dreadful. In my mind I knew this time was different.

It took about an hour to get to the hospital. Ronnie continued to try to calm my fears, but to no avail. Odd as it sounds, I did most of the talking—probably because of my nerves. But some of the stuff I said didn't make sense.

"I know God is in this, and He has done something. Ronnie, I'm all prayed up, and I know God wouldn't let anything enter my life without Him being a part of what's happening." I rambled on and on.

"I'm sure you're right, Sharon," he nodded in an effort to appease me.

"You may find this odd, but I've never read the Bible like I should—I know so little about it and find it hard to understand, but I've always had a good relationship with God, and He has revealed Himself continually to me all through my Christian life.

"Do you find that strange? Perhaps to a preacher that sounds odd, but it's how it has been in my life. I've prayed to God since I was thirteen years old, and He answers. But I struggle with understanding the Bible. Does that make sense to you?

"Please believe me when I say that God has done something tonight. He would never leave me all alone. Plus, I've prayed for Wally's salvation for, well, I don't know how many years, but a long, long time. I know God did something," I stated with complete confidence.

"When this is over you'll see that God is in on this, and He's done something." I continued to make these kinds of statements again and again as we raced toward the hospital, and I don't know why I said them because neither of us knew anything at all about the accident. Positive comments continued to roll off my tongue about how God was in control and had done something. It was surreal. Each time I proclaimed that God was in charge, Ronnie would strive to keep me calm. I think he thought I was losing it. My words indicated, however, that it was a grave situation, and Ronnie didn't see it that way. I would have loved to have seen it his way, but I knew Wally. When he was in an accident, *he always called me*—not someone else.

At the time I didn't realize how it sounded to Ronnie. But he was patient. I had absolutely no doubt in my mind that God was on the scene. For some reason a giant faith emerged in me. I truly needed it at that moment, and this story reveals God's amazing power. This unusual, elevated experience of faith empowered me.

As I entered the side door of the emergency room at the hospital late that night, I saw my mother first. Shock and agony registered on her face. Tears streaming down her cheeks from swollen, red eyes. She grabbed me and held me close. At that moment I knew I was right. All doubt was erased. This was serious. The next thing I remember was sitting down in a folding chair and my dad kneeling down directly in front of me, tears running down his cheeks, and stroking my hand. The scene was a solemn one. They said nothing, but their countenance told me my worst fears were true. They mirrored trepidation and anguish. Thoughts raced through my mind. Wally was critical, and I couldn't bear to see him. *Could I handle it?* I wondered. Not now. He had left home so healthy, but now what? I tried to be brave, but I couldn't do it. *Let me get myself together*, I thought, *and then I can face reality and comfort him. I'm no good to anyone if I'm falling apart. Time, I need time.*

I barely remember the things that happened next. Soon someone led me down a long hallway, but I struggled to get away. "No, I can't see him right now!" I yelled as I pulled away from their grip. "Don't take me where he is please!" I pleaded in a horrified tone of voice. I continued to be led against my will. Why would they take me to his room and make me witness some horrible sight when I wasn't prepared? I needed time to let things soak in first. My mind raced with these thoughts, yet, they continued to propel me forward as I tried to pull back.

Eventually they drug me down the hall. I knew I would fall apart if I walked in and he was hooked up to machines, all bloody and perhaps dismembered. I couldn't understand why they were forcing me there without listening to one thing I had to say—and they said nothing.

The next thing I knew they led me into a tiny room that contained one small desk in the corner and perhaps a couple of chairs in front of it. A drab, tiny room with no pictures or plaques of any kind. The walls were bare. It was obviously a room used for nothing. My mother sat me in a chair. There were others present, but I don't remember who. Straight away a man wearing a white lab coat came through a side door. He leaned on the side of the desk and asked which one of us was Mrs. Stephenson. His manner was blunt, cold, and routine.

"I'm Mrs. Stephenson," I answered in a soft, weak voice.

"Well, Mrs. Stephenson, I want you to know that Mr. Stephenson did not suffer. I also need to know which funeral home you plan to use so we can transfer his body there." He stated in a monotone voice with absolutely no feeling.

I leaped out of my chair, ran past the door, and found myself in another large, empty waiting room. I sat down and stared straight ahead. Mother followed me out the door. I glanced up at her and said, "Will you please tell him what he needs to know? I don't ... no, I can't say another word."

The world was different. I spoke with no expression, for the "me" inside this body was gone. My mother must have taken care of everything, I really don't know. I was somewhere between fantasy and reality. Now, as I reflect upon the scene, surely this doctor had assumed my parents had already informed me. He had a job to do, but I wasn't aware that breaking the sad news of the death of my husband belonged to him. I'm positive he never meant to be unsympathetic toward me. I believe my mother and father loved Wally so much they couldn't bring themselves to say it. I blame no one. The outcome would have been the same no matter who told me. Wally was gone, and it took a long time to sink in.

Mother and I decided to ride back with Ronnie. Reality is, she went with me everywhere. She began an all out effort to keep me sane. We went to the restroom as if life was normal. I had in my hand a death certificate. It listed cause of death as shock. There it was in black and white—D.O.A. (Dead On Arrival). Surely not. I'd just kissed him goodbye less than three hours ago. Now a little piece of paper informed me he was dead. That didn't make it real for me. I was mute. All the talking I'd done before ceased. There was dead silence on our way back home. I didn't realize it, but I had sunk into another world. A world I'd never been in before. It was dark, mysterious, and unfamiliar. When we arrived at my house, Ronnie came in to get his family. They had strange looks on their faces, but no one said a word. Finally,

Ronnie asked if we could pray.

"Sure, that would be good," I replied weakly. I don't know what he said; I didn't hear it. My mind was centered on our house, which we had spent the last five years restoring as a family. They left and I was alone with my parents and children to sort things out. Intermittently I wandered in and out of my children's room as they lay sleeping. Unaware that they now had no father, they slept peacefully until morning. *How will I ever tell them?* Mark was almost two years old. He'd have no clue what was happening. But Kerrie and Stevie's lives would be forever changed, and I was helpless concerning the onslaught of pain that they were able to endure.

My mom and dad paced the floor all night. They spoke in whispers about legalities of the wreck. Was it Wally's fault? What had happened, when and where? Finally, I could take no more. I asked them as politely as possible not to speak of it anymore that night. The house fell into silence.

As the sun rose on a brand new day, I was barely aware that my heart still beat. One thing scared me, strange as it might sound, but I had not cried one time. Somehow that didn't seem normal to me. Why had I not shed one tear? Everything appeared to be moving in slow motion. I was numb. It's natural to cry when a loved one dies. So while lying on the couch, I silently spoke to God. *Please help me think of something that will cause me to cry. I'm hurting so bad inside. I also have one more wish. Please take me out of this world until I can handle this disaster.*

I didn't realize God had already taken me out of the world and placed a shield around me. Instantly, I began to cry as thoughts bombarded my mind. I thought about our plans—the great year we'd had when he was off work due to his finger. Our family had became so close. As good, meaningful thoughts rushed through my brain, the tears began to flow. Overwhelming release washed over me.

The telephone rang around 6:00 a.m. It was *The Cleburne Times Review*. They needed to write the obituary. As I answered all their questions, I realized my emotions were lying deep within me and did not necessarily surface because I spoke the facts. The answers seemed to come from someone else—not me. I moved and spoke like a robot.

The kids were still asleep, and I walked in and out of their rooms, but the difference now was that I shed tears easily. I had many questions. How would they ever remember their father? They were so young. I prayed hard. *God, You have to come through for all of us. My children will have pain just as I'm hurting now, and I'm powerless and defenseless in guarding them from it.* A mother's job it to protect her children. It's a natural instinct. But I couldn't change anything.

Ronnie had promised he would come and help me tell the children. When they woke up, they knew something didn't seem right. Ronnie began, "Last night your daddy was in a bad wreck, but the good news is that you will see him again when Jesus comes back and we all go to heaven," he endeavored to explain in a childlike manner.

They looked at me and then looked back at him. It wasn't sinking in. Kerrie was seven, and she caught on first. She knew something bad had happened to her daddy. Tears gathered in her eyes. Stevie was five and looked puzzled. Mark almost two sat in my lap and simply wanted this stranger to leave our house. I didn't know until later that Stevie thought that God had taken their daddy away.

The following day I heard Stevie screaming in his room and kicking the walls. When I came in, his anger was quite visible. "Stevie, what's wrong?" I asked.

"I hate God. He took my daddy away. The preacher said so. God's not nice at all," he yelled while kicking his feet against the wall.

"Stevie, God loved your father. Sometimes we lose someone even when they're young. I know God had a reason for all this."

"I don't care. I hate God. He needs to bring my daddy back. I hate Him; I hate Him," he screamed as he continued to kick his feet against the wall. What could I say? I continued to try to comfort him, but it was to no avail. Kerrie was like me, she just cried and stared in confusion. As for Mark, my mother sent him to Susan's house, and I never even knew it. I'd taken care of Mark since his birth, and now I didn't even ask where my baby was. It was obvious; I wasn't all there. But I trusted the people around me to take care of everything and everyone—and they did.

Weary from the events since the accident, my eyelids closed automatically. When someone spoke to me they opened, otherwise they were closed. However, my mood had changed. A tranquil, calm spirit engulfed me. A thought or memory, "a still, small voice," reminded my troubled brain, "Thou wilt keep him in perfect peace whose mind is stayed on thee" (Isa. 26:3, KJV). I coveted this peace in me, for suddenly our home was anything but normal. People came from everywhere. Several ladies came from church and busied themselves in my kitchen preparing meals. They went upstairs and cleaned Wally's room—even washing his clothes. I'd never seen so much food and plenty of people to eat it. This was no longer my home. I felt out of place here. All chores were taken over by someone else—people who had never even been in my home.

Periodically someone would urge me to come to the table and eat. But I couldn't. Perhaps I drank tea, coffee, or something, I don't remember. I was somewhere else in my own private world. That was good. Strangers answered my telephone. People went in and out as if I wasn't there. There's no doubt, others were completely taking care of me.

The only one I was aware of was my mother. I didn't struggle; I simply trusted. I have great admiration for the mother God gave me. She became my right-hand person. Wally's life insurance concerned her, not me. So she dug through piles of bills and papers and located what was needed. I drifted through the next two days. My mother guided me, thought for me, moved for me. Absolutely nothing entered into my brain.

Conversely, I continued to tell everyone the same things I had expressed to Ronnie on the way to the hospital before I knew Wally's life had ended. I was positive beyond any doubt that God had done something and would reveal it to me at some point in time. I asserted this tremendous faith and never with any understanding. Everyone who crossed my path and heard about it, shook their heads, and patted my hands. I know what they were thinking. "Whatever you say, Sharon" or "She'll be okay later." I was being patronized. But none of this swayed me. I told everyone these words with strong conviction, yet nothing had happened. We all knew Wally had died. That's all.

A few years later, someone explained to me that my family thought I was close to a nervous breakdown. It certainly appeared so. Everyone was patient with me and pampered me, but they watched intently. But let's face it. Clearly Wally had died in a terrible accident—I had lost my husband and the children their father. Nothing good had happened. Yet, I was positively proclaiming God had done something great and He would let us know what it was in time. God was faithful; God was good and loving. I knew Him and knew He had to be involved. My mother-in-law approached my mom about putting me in the hospital. She was gravely concerned for my welfare for what I was saying manifested no logic at all. To everyone else Wally's untimely death was a dreadful mistake.

But my faith was strong: "Now faith is the assurance of things hoped for, the conviction of things not seen" (Heb. 11:1).

God gives gifts and perhaps He gives them in greater measure when we need them most. I've always thought, without really understanding it, that this unusual faith came from God. It had nothing to do with me. I'd known God long enough to fully trust Him regarding Wally's death. God had never failed me—why would He now at such a vulnerable time.

It took some time, but the story unfolded slowly, deliberately, and fully just as I had stated it would. God showed up and answered loud and clear.

Professionals tell us that everyone needs some kind of closure, one of those psychology words that is a bit overused sometimes. Perhaps there's some truth. I know it took a while. I feel nutty even writing this feeling, but it was true. I was angry. He was supposed to be with us. He loved us. These thoughts would come especially at night. He was supposed to be home. He was mine, and he was gone. I wanted answers. Looking back—to me he was still alive, just not home where he should be. Like my five year old, I wanted him back. Death is a difficult reality. I had no warning—no preparation. He just couldn't be gone forever, I concluded. That wasn't possible in my heart.

I really became quite childlike. I couldn't close the bathroom door without fear. My mother asked me to go to the car one night to get a piece of paper we needed, and I couldn't go out in the dark. I tried to sleep at my house one night, but I heard noises all night. That didn't happen again.

Funeral arrangements were complete. On Sunday my Aunt Charlotte encouraged me to go and see Wally. I had decided I would not do that—I wanted to remember him alive. After much coercing, she finally talked me into it. He wore his yellow shirt and brown tie and looked so peaceful. I remember feeling a heaviness in my chest—I could barely breathe. Two people escorted me out because I almost fainted. It was the first realness I'd seen. It was too much. Tears flowed as my body crumpled to the floor. I'd never experienced grief so severe. I didn't even understand the word until it crushed my heart like a bulldozer.

I'm so sorry I didn't take Kerrie and Stevie. I was trying to protect them. Hindsight is 20/20. They had a right to see their father—have a better understanding of death. Another one of my many mistakes. My daddy's mouth quivered with great difficulty and he held back a sob when Stevie asked him at the graveside, "Granddaddy, is my daddy in that box?"

I gave Ronnie several verses I felt were appropriate. One was from Ecclesiastes 3, which tells us there is a season for everything: There's a time to be born and a time to die (verse 2). The funeral home called and informed me of the music selection. I hung up and immediately cringed. The songs were old and very sad. At mother's beckoning I phoned them and changed all the music. There were to be happy songs only. One song was "How Great Thou Art," which Elvis Presley had made famous. Wally's favorite hymn had always been "Mansions Over the Hilltop." I knew we had to praise God for what He'd done in our lives. Although, as of yet, we still weren't sure what that was.

Finally, it was time for the funeral. My throat ached as I held back unwanted tears. I determined to be strong until I looked over at Kerrie. Little tears streamed down her face. I couldn't look any longer. If I did I'd be in trouble. My child was hurting, and I couldn't comfort her. We would both fall apart.

After the funeral several of my longtime friends from high school spoke with me. They claimed it was one of the most uplifting funerals they'd witnessed. I was glad. For in the back of my mind there would be something special to praise God about—I continued to believe. When we arrived home the ladies from my church had prepared lunch. Jean Shelton seemed to be in charge. She and I were Sunday school co-teachers.

Jean told me about a strange telephone call while we were at the funeral. This woman was afraid she had called the wrong number the evening Wally died, and she had called back to be certain of reaching the right person. Wally was a small man, and she had thought he was only a teenager. With the helmet on his head she couldn't tell his age. This mysterious caller left her phone number and address in case I wanted to contact her. She was the one who had held his hand when he passed away. Her name was Cecilia Clark, and she lived one or two blocks from the site of the accident. Jean scribbled the number onto my phone book. I told her we would probably visit to find out a bit more of what happened that night.

I kept believing that God was going to somehow make everything all right in the end. In His time He would let us in on it. And in actuality He was already working behind the scenes while thoughts raced through my mind.

I was so glad Mother was there to think for me. I was exhausted, yet there was so much business that needed to be taken care of. For starters, we had to go to the police station in Burleson in order to obtain the accident report. Next, I had to sign papers to turn the motorcycle over to the insurance company. Then, we had to make an appointment with the Social Security Board to inform them of Wally's death. My parents informed me that the kids would be taken care of by way of Social Security funds so I could stay home and raise them.

"Oh, by the way, Mom, we need to visit that lady, Cecilia Clark, who was at the scene of the accident. She lives in Burleson. Let's call her and see if we can drop by while we're in Burleson taking care of business," I suggested.

"Yeah, that's a good idea. Maybe she can tell us more about the accident than what we'll see on paper. Didn't she say she was there holding his hand, or something like that?"

"I know, I'm curious about what all she had to do with it," I said. "I'm anxious to know if Wally said anything to her. So let's go talk to her as soon as possible. I'll give her a call right now!"

The more we discussed it, the more inquisitive we became. She had been an eyewitness. As we drove into Burleson we reached our destination, but we couldn't find the police station. We stopped at a gas station just a few feet from the accident site to get directions.

"Are you the lady whose husband got killed just down the street?" a man asked me.

"Yes," I informed him.

"Well, I'm sure sorry 'bout that. You know, they completely stopped traffic on this highway after it happened. There was lots of people gathered 'round him—closed the whole rode off. Bad accident, you know." He continued filling me in on more than I really was prepared to hear. But he didn't know that.

At the police station they gave me detailed information concerning the accident. They had it drawn out on paper. It was far from easy to view, but fortunately it was no ones fault. They called it a "freak" or "no-fault" accident. A young man's brakes went out on his car, and he ran a stop sign from a side rode onto the highway and hit Wally. We called his home and assured them that we had no ill thoughts toward them. It was simply an accident. We were glad he was not hurt.

We at last succeeded in completing the business and proceeded to Cecilia's house, excited about meeting her. We turned right just after a convenience store and into a residential area. We surmised she must have been at the store to get to Wally so promptly that fateful evening. Her house was at the end of the road about a block from the store.

Mother and I entered her home and sat down in her small living area. It was so small her husband and children stood in the doorway and along the wall. I sat near Cecilia on the divan, and Mother sat in a chair directly across from me. We anticipated condolences from this family, but that is not what happened. I was anxious to talk with her and hear details concerning the accident. After introductions and small talk, she began to speak about holding Wally's hand. The conversation immediately took on a more serious tone.

"Nothing like this has ever happened to me," she began. I sensed her anguish. One could tell she didn't know how to commence. But rapidly my heart began to pound as I realized this was not to be a normal gathering. Mother and I sensed the Holy Spirit leading her conversation.

She and her husband had been preparing for bed late Friday night, she began telling us, when they both heard a loud crash. It was obvious to them it was close by. She automatically grabbed her robe and raced out onto the front lawn to see what the commotion was about. Her husband realized she had plans to run down the street in the middle of the night, so he told her to wait and he would get the car.

"No! I can't wait, I have to go now," she yelled emphatically. She didn't even wait for an answer. When she reached the scene of the accident, she looked around and nobody was doing anything. Someone had placed a blanket on Wally, but he lay there in the middle of the road bleeding and completely alone. She suddenly felt compelled to go over to him and hold his hand. "Compelled" was the exact word she used, driven by some force within. She claimed that normally she couldn't even help her children when it involved blood. But God had led her to be with Wally, and she knew she must go. As she stared in disbelief, the only thing she knew to do was to pray. He was alive, and she knew it. She didn't know anything of his spiritual status, so she began to ask him if he knew Jesus. Again and again she asked him if he knew Jesus as she prayed for his salvation. She sensed he would not be a part of this world much longer. That was obvious. The crowd watched in amazement as this tiny woman prayed and prayed and proclaimed the name of Jesus to this badly wounded man. There was no wailing or groaning or cries of distress from Wally. He was so weak; he could not speak. She continued to pray for Wally in his final moments of life.

She asked me if she could hold my hand as she explained further. We clasped hands, and with tears in everyone's eyes, I knew God was there. My mother is not a crier, but she was weeping, tears streaming down her cheeks. Cecilia spoke softly but with a confidence and authority that was uncanny. She asked me if I was worried about Wally's salvation. I looked at my mom when I answered, "Yes, for a long time."

"Well," Cecilia began, "God spoke to me as I prayed, and His communication was clear. Your husband is right with his Creator. You will see him again! God heard all your prayers and answered."

If anyone knew my concern for Wally, it was my mother. She knew he always assured me he was a Christian, but he never lived the life or went to church with me. He would not even discuss it without becoming defensive and angry. She was aware of my deep concern for his salvation. Now we both knew what God had placed in my heart from the moment I'd received a call from Cecilia that Friday night around 11:40 p.m. He had died around 10:50, but God was in control and sent a messenger in the form of Cecilia. Now my heart could cry out as David did in Psalms 42. God is my hope, joy, and salvation. I see His lovingkindness in the daytime, and I have a song at night. My hope is in God, my Rock, and I shall yet praise Him. He did not forget me, and He did not forget Wally. I had my answer I'd waited so long for. God knew when and how and through whom to bring this great news to me.

No words will ever clarify what took place in this small room. How I wish I had some magical words to spread on this paper that would adequately describe what we all experienced that day as we shared in the sadness of death mixed with the joy of salvation.

There's an interesting story in the Bible about a man who was blind from birth. Jesus restored his sight, and he was so excited that he told everyone who would listen. The pretentious religious groups of that day questioned him as to who did this thing to him. They even made it sound like an evil act. His reply was so simple. "I don't really know who Jesus is, all I know is this; I was blind and now I see."

When things of a great magnitude occur in our lives, sometimes like the blind man, we are excited, awed, and thankful—we accept it readily and willingly with no reservations. We don't know all of the whys and hows, and we really don't care. It happened and that's all that matters to us.

Well, like the blind man, I knew Jesus had saved Wally, and it didn't matter to me how, just that He did. God had done something. Here it was—the answer I had waited for. What could I say? God hadn't let me down. I wanted to tell the whole world. Somehow I knew even before I was aware that Wally was dead that God had done something. I had faith in God, like many others in Hebrews 11. God always honors faith!

Satan comes to rob and steal from us. He tried to make me believe it was all a lie. God lied to me, so I would be happy for the rest of my life instead of discouraged. God revealed to me that the Bible states clearly that Satan is the father of all lies. God gives us a choice—to believe and have faith, or not. Jesus saved Wally that night completely and forever.

This is who the Bible says Jesus is: "Jesus, on the other hand, because He continues forever, holds His priesthood permanently. Therefore He is able also to save forever those who draw near to God through Him, since He always lives to make intercession for them" (Heb. 7:24, 25).

When Jesus went home to be with the Father, He left the front door open, and all who accept Him are welcome and will one day live with Him forever when He returns to take everyone home with Him.

The very moment I walked through the door of my mother's house, I wanted to find God, so I went straight to the Bible. I didn't know what else to do, but I was walking on air—I was so excited. Remember, I knew little of the Bible, but I knew God, so I opened it up and pointed to Psalms 40, and this is what I read: "I waited patiently for the Lord; and He inclined to me and heard my cry. He brought me up out of the pit of destruction, out of the miry clay, and He set my feet upon a rock making my footsteps firm. He put a new song in my mouth, a song of praise to our God; many will see and fear, and will trust in the Lord. How blessed is the man who has made the Lord his trust ... Many, O Lord my God, are the wonders which You have done, and Your thoughts toward us; There is none to compare with You. If I would declare and speak of them, they would be too numerous to count" (verse 1–5).

Many people heard about the accident. I discovered later that two young men accepted Jesus into their lives in Rio Vista because of it. One of them rode a motorcycle every day to work. He didn't let the preacher leave until he knew he was saved. Many people who had watched Cecilia pray with Wally were friends with someone in Rio Vista. At church I heard it made quite an impression upon a lot of people who were there.

What happened to Wally reminds me of another great story in the Bible I just recently found. Satan never leaves us alone, but if you believe in the Bible, that it's God's Word, then it's not hard to believe God can do today what He did a long time ago. This story took place in A.D. 62. This story has to be told in its entirety:

"An angel of the Lord spoke to Philip saying, 'Get up and go south to the road that descends from Jerusalem to Gaza.' (This is a desert road.) So he got up and went; and there was an Ethiopian eunuch, a court official of Candace, queen of the Ethiopians, who was in charge of all her treasure; and he had come to Jerusalem to worship, and he was returning and sitting in his chariot, and was reading the prophet Isaiah. Then the Spirit said to Philip, 'Go up and join this chariot.' Philip ran up and heard him reading Isaiah the prophet, and said, 'Do you understand what you are reading?' And he said, 'Well, how could I, unless someone guides me?' And he invited Philip to come up and sit with him. Now the passage of Scripture which he was reading was this:

'He was led as a sheep to slaughter;
And as a Lamb before its shearer is silent,
So He does not open His mouth,
'In humiliation His judgment was taken away;
Who shall relate His generation?
For His life is removed from the earth.'

"And the eunuch answered Philip and said, 'Please tell me, of whom does the prophet say this? Of himself or of someone else?' Then Philip opened his mouth, and beginning from this Scripture he preached Jesus to him. As they went along the road they came to some water; and the eunuch said, 'Look! Water! What prevents me from being baptized?' And Philip said, 'If you believe with all your heart, you may.' And he answered and said, 'I believe that Jesus Christ is the Son of God.' And he ordered the chariot to stop; and they both went down into the water, Philip as well as the eunuch, and he baptized him" (Acts 8:26–38).

Philip went where he was needed just at the moment he was needed. History tells us that the Ethiopian went back to his country and started a church where thousands learned of Jesus. Philip had a divine appointment to save one man. He was faithful to God's calling.

We never want to wait upon the Lord. We think we can work things out on our own initiative. I saw all kinds of ways God could have saved Wally. I'd seen countless wives get their husbands to the altar and accept Jesus, but it never happened for me. Because of my personality, I came down hard upon Wally at times. This may seem crazy, but I thought if I yelled and screamed the Bible at him (pretty much hit him over the head with the Bible) I could change him myself. Just before his death, he began to work a second shift at the railroad with one of our deacons from our church. I started to tell God—this could be the way. I asked Wally one evening if he liked his new coworker. He exclaimed rudely what I didn't want to hear. He couldn't stand him—he thought he was stuck up. So there went that plan. My heart sunk. Wally was so mad at me for browbeating him that he finally told me not to talk to him about God ever again. Now, I had really done it. So I began praying that God would send someone he would listen to. I had no idea He would answer the way He did—sending someone down the road in the middle of the night. But that's exactly what He did.

It's been a lot of years, but I still miss him. Yet there is hope. Jesus conquered death for us, and He has the keys to death and hell, which the Bible tells us in Revelation 1:18. We all have lost someone close to us because of death. Kerrie recently sent me a poem that I'd like to share.

Life is fragile—we need to take it more seriously. God says our life is like a vapor, here for a moment, then gone. King David said it so well in Psalm when he asked God to help him to number his days. We have such a short time here on earth.

"If I knew it would be the last time that I'd see you fall asleep, I would tuck you in more tightly and pray the Lord, your soul to keep.

"If I knew it would be the last time that I'd see you walk out the door, I would give you a hug and kiss and call you back for one more.

"If I knew it would be the last time I'd hear your voice lifted up in praise, I would videotape each action and word, so I could play them back day after day.

"If I knew it would be the last time, I could spare an extra minute or two to stop and say, 'I love you,' instead of assuming you would KNOW I do.

"If I knew it would be the last time I would be there to share your day, well I'm sure you'll have so many more, so I can let just this one slip away, for surely there's always tomorrow to make up for an oversight, and we always get a second chance to make everything right.

"There will always be another day to say our 'I love you's' and certainly there's another chance to say our 'anything I can do's'?

"But just in case I might be wrong and today is all I get I'd like to say how much I love you and hope we never forget.

"Tomorrow is not promised to anyone, young or old alike, and today may be the last chance you get to hold your loved one tight.

"So if you're waiting for tomorrow, why not do it

today? For if tomorrow never comes, you'll surely regret the day that you didn't take that extra time for a smile, a hug, or a kiss, and you were too busy to grant someone what turned out to be their one last wish.

"So hold your loved ones close today and whisper in their ear. Tell them how much you love them and that you'll always hold them dear

"Take time to say 'I'm sorry,' 'Please forgive me,' 'Thank you,' or 'It's okay.' And if tomorrow never comes, you'll have no regrets about today"

(Author Unknown).

Chapter Nine

Light of the Morning

Isaiah 60:20 says, "Your sun will no longer set, nor will your moon wane; for you will have the Lord for an everlasting light, and the days of your mourning will be over." In our darkest night, God is our everlasting light, breaking through and bringing a new day and light for our way. Jesus is a light that will never go out. His light triumphs over darkness in the world—and in us.

Many years ago at a Bible conference, the late Dr. D. M. Stearns held a question and answer session at which the following question was asked:

"If you had prayed all your life for the salvation of a loved one, and then you got word that that person had died without giving any evidence of repentance—having lived a sinful life—what would you think, both of prayer itself and of the love of God and His promise to answer?"

It was a striking question, and everyone in the room wondered how he would respond. Then he told this story: A young service man named Brad was hitchhiking when Lew Masters, a real estate broker, picked him up. As they rode along, Brad led this businessman to receive Christ as his Savior. Out of much appreciation, the older man gave Brad his card as they were about to part, urging him to look him up if he was ever in Chicago.

Five years passed before Brad had opportunity to visit Chicago and accept the invitation. And this was his amazing discovery: only a few minutes after they had parted that day, Lew had been killed in an auto accident.

Now, you can hardly imagine Mrs. Masters' joy when she heard from Brad how her husband had received Christ as his Savior just before his death. She said, "I had walked with Christ for many years and had prayed for my husband often. When he was killed, I thought God had not answered my prayers. Now for five years I've been out of fellowship with God—all because I thought He had failed me"

God alone knows the last chapter, and just like in my case, He chooses to reveal it in His time. No one can understand God's timing. I'm so grateful He didn't make me wait five years.

One morning as we were sipping coffee, Mother and I discussed as many of the details we could remember about Cecilia's talk with us. Cecilia had difficulty explaining certain details to us, so she at one point had used an analogy. She felt like God had used her like a bridge to help Wally find the way to God by her bringing Jesus on the scene. I told Mother I didn't remember much about what Ronnie had said at the funeral, but Mother remembered that he spoke of bridges all along the way of life.

"Sharon, these are the exact words Cecilia used. She was the bridge helping Wally come to Jesus," Mother replied.

"Maybe you're right, Mother. I just can't remember—I heard very little at the funeral," I explained.

"You know something? The funeral home gave you a little book. I bet Ronnie's notes are in it. Why don't you bring it to the table, and we'll look through it and see." I quickly ran to locate the book to see if Ronnie had placed his sermon notes inside. Mother and I scanned the pages, and there it was. He was a good speaker, so all he had written on paper was "bridges all along the way." He and Cecilia had used the same words.

Each morning the minute I woke up and my mind was alert, it would hit me that Wally was not there anymore. It struck my brain like a nail, and it hurt. Then instantly I'd think about what Wally and I had spoken about the night before he died. The article about the girl on the tracks haunted me. But I couldn't understand why. I prayed every morning, asking God for peace about the article and the moments of the night before his death, but no answer came. Something told me the article and Wally's death were significant, but I was in a spiritual fog, if you will. Morning after morning I woke early, the sun was bright, but my mind was in the dark. It was as if something prompted me immediately after I awoke to think of the girl on the tracks. I couldn't shake the importance of it. Again, God revealed it in His timing. After three or four days the Holy Spirit finally spoke loud and clear. It reminded me of Job when God began to speak to him. Sometimes when I read Job, it makes me feel that God's angry with him. But that's not the case. When God speaks, He doesn't mince words. He tells it like it is, straightforward.

I wondered why I was so blind. Wally's death was somehow tied to that story—a little girl's close encounter with death. God must show one the answer because spiritual things are always discerned spiritually. When God troubles the heart, He will reveal truth. After several days my eyes were opened to God's reality. Suddenly it was crystal clear.

You know how the little girl was saved by a mere man in only a matter of seconds? God spoke to me in my thoughts. *Why would you not realize that I, God, could save Wally? My timing is perfect, and I can save someone completely and forever in a matter of seconds. Can I not do even beyond what a mere man can do? I saved Wally that night in a matter of seconds and sealed his soul for all eternity. If man can do amazing things and you stand in awe of them, why would you not believe that God also can do amazing things?*

In Genesis 18:14 it asks the question, "Is anything too difficult for the Lord?" and in Jeremiah 32:17 it says, "Nothing is too difficult for You." Jesus told us that all things are possible with God.

Then I remembered that the man in the article had stated that he felt compelled to help the little girl while everyone else stood by horrified. Cecilia had used the same exact words concerning

Wally. The man in the subway station had saved the little girl's life in seconds. Cecilia had raced to the scene compelled to pray with Wally, and she became the bridge that brought him to Jesus. She, too, had only seconds. Wally had passed away by the time the ambulance arrived. His death certificate stated he died of shock. This is a calm death for the person simply goes to sleep. But the last thing to leave someone who is dying is the hearing. He heard Cecilia praying for him and calling on Jesus. Scripture tells us that "whosoever shall call upon the name of the Lord shall be saved" (Rom. 10:13, NIV).

Unlike the man in the article, Cecilia got no public tribute, but in heaven one day she will get God's reward.

One evening I was looking for a verse in the Bible that was a specific promise for God's children, but I didn't have a clue where I'd seen it. I'd searched for it through all my references, but I couldn't find it. I went to bed disappointed that I didn't know what book I'd found it in. My mother came to my bedside around 10:30 p.m. and said, "If God doesn't stop doing things, I don't know if I can take it." She had opened her little Jerusalem Bible my aunt had bought for her from a trip to the Holy Land. It was marked with the red ribbon in Romans. I knew I hadn't used that Bible because the print was so small. She scanned the page and there it was, the promise I had been looking for: "God causes all things to work together for good to those who love God, to those who are called according to His purpose" (Rom. 8:28).

You would have to know my mother to understand how odd all this was for her. She loved Jesus but had always had a quiet walk with Him. Her nature was to help others and to unconditionally love everyone in her path. This saying by St. Francis of Assisi epitomizes my mother's life: "Preach Jesus every day, and if necessary use words." I'm glad my mother was seeing all that God was doing. I tend to be a bit more exotic, eccentric, and sometimes extreme when it comes to God, but my mother toned me down. However, we both saw His hand in everything, and it made a deep impression on her. Otherwise, I might have thought I was crazy.

Each morning I would wake up way before anyone else. I would slip quietly out of bed, curl up in a lounge chair near a window and enjoy the morning sun streaming in. One morning I found another *Reader's Digest* article that looked interesting. The title of the article was "There Came a Cry of Joy." This story won an award for its unusual style, but I will endeavor to tell it in my often long and boring manner.

A man was sent on a mission to a valley surrounded by magnificent, stately mountains in order to capture some birds, reptiles, or anything to restock a zoo. He entered an old, rundown cabin, and there he found a number of hawks inside. Managing to grab hold of one of them, he noticed the hawks mate found an avenue to escape. However, he had effectively captured a sparrow hawk, a fine young male in the prime of his life. As the young hunter prepared the cage to transport this special cargo to the zoo, he noticed the hawk continually gazed upward toward the sky.

The man was curious about what his victim saw high above them, so he began to search the blue skies for the answer. As he scanned the firmament, he noticed the mate circling high above in the clouds. When he spotted her, he could not believe the nightmarish, harsh loud cry and noisy protest she made directly above them. He had never heard such an awful, disturbing sound. He no longer felt honorable about what he was supposed to do. He knew he would probably choose to abort this mission. After much deliberation, he allowed the captured bird to go free, and the hawk flew into the sky to be with his mate. It wasn't so much what the young man saw that stunned him, but what he heard high above the earth in the clear blue heavens. There came a cry of such unutterable and ecstatic joy that he claimed, he never got over it. "They met each other and soared into the upper regions way beyond the eyes of men," the author stated at the end of the story (Loren Eiseley, "There Came A Cry of Joy," February 1977, pp. 97–99).

As I knelt in prayer, I thought, *On earth Wally was limited and sometimes in intense pain. Someday in the future I will be reunited with Wally, and we will live with our Maker forever.* Our real purpose and destination is to be with God. We view this world differently when we understand this concept.

A picture always belongs to the artist, a song belongs to its composer, a poem belongs to the author, an invention to the inventor, and a creator its creation. We think of death as a robber of something we loved. But God says: "Precious in the sight of the Lord is the death of His godly ones" (Ps. 116:15).

I continued to wake up early, and one morning I read another *Reader's Digest* article. (By the way, I've finally learned how to read the Bible through with understanding. Since I'm a little ADD I read one book at a time carefully, slowly, and meaningfully. After all, the Bible is sixty-six books written at different times and by various authors. That made sense to me, and it works.)

The next story was about a young girl who at the age of twenty-two died of pressure on the brain. Five years prior to her death, she had sketched a portrait of her dream man. She enjoyed drawing and writing poetry. Her death was tragic for her family—she had so many plans in life and was so young. Her parents made a difficult choice. They donated a cornea from one of her eyes to a young man stricken with blindness. The recipient strikingly resembled the man of her dreams in the picture she had sketched. When he visited her parents, he was surprised to see this sketch hanging on the wall of their home. He was taken aback by how closely it resembled him. Even odder, underneath the mysterious picture was a poem she had written about life and death. "Of anguish, none is greater than the passing of two hearts that never knew each other" (Carl Bakal, "Linda's Haunting Vision," February 1977, pp. 68–72).

These words spoke clearly to me. That is what happened between Wally and Cecilia. They would never know each other here, yet they had met at the most critical moment of Wally's life—the culmination of it. It was a brief acquaintance, but what a way to go—someone whispering Jesus in your ear and holding tightly to your hand while praying for your soul.

About a month after Wally's death, I had a perplexing and disturbing dream that was surreal. Wally was in the room and I urged him to come to me. He looked scared. I asked him to give me one last kiss and to hug me, but he only shook his head back and forth as if to say he couldn't grant me my wish. In seconds I felt his lips on mine, and then the dream made a sound—*poof!*

I woke up shaking and my heart pounding. The dream had been so real it was as if it had actually happened. I was afraid. That same day Susan and I had been in Fort Worth at a mall shopping when we ran into Cecilia. I entreated her to let me come by again to see if she could recall anymore about what had happened. I wanted more and more of the story, but there was no more. However, God understood what was in my heart.

"Sharon, what I told you is all I know," Cecilia explained. "That is what God told me to tell you. I have no idea how God did it. I wish I could say more," she patiently and kindly explained, "but there isn't anything else to tell you."

I was disappointed, but in reality I didn't want the high to go away—kind of like Peter when Jesus was transfigured and was seen talking with Elijah and Moses in Matthew 17. Peter was on a high, and he didn't want to come down. However, as Peter learned, we have to leave the mountaintop and come back down to live life in this dark, difficult, often lonely world.

The events that took place and all that encompassed Wally's death were a benchmark in my Christian experience. I learned a lot about God while walking with Him. The last year God gave us together was more special than I'd realized at the time. Wally's near loss of his finger gave us one year together that drew us all closer—all five of us. It was like Ronnie Millsap's song "It Was Almost Like a Song." It ended far too soon, but I had soft, precious memories because of it.

As I have finally become a better student of the Bible, I've discovered God does have a plan for wives whose husbands are not saved. "You wives, be submissive to your own husbands so that even if any of them are disobedient to the word, they may be won without a word by the behavior of their wives, as they observe your chaste and respectful behavior.... but let it be the hidden person of the heart, with the imperishable quality of a gentle and quiet spirit, which is precious in the sight of God" (1 Peter 3:1–5).

I'm sorry I didn't know this. I was mean and ugly, but my heart and motives were right. Much of the time my actions were inappropriate, yet God still listened to me. I should have known what an awful personality I had inherited when my younger brother, Drew, proclaimed every time someone asked him what he wanted to be when he grew up, "I want to be mean and skinny like Sharon!" I guess that says it all. There was ten years between us, so Drew was only two or three at the time. We thought it was so cute.

I'm not sure how each detail was accomplished, but the last night Wally and I had together was anything but normal. Something caused our spirits to meet. He sensed strongly that something was wrong with me, and he, in some mysterious way, seemed to be aware of my depression. He leaned over and kissed me goodbye and told me he loved me. He turned around before walking out of the door—out of my life forever here on earth—and simply, softly, and sweetly said, "I'll see you in the morning, Honey." It has been thirty-three years since his death, and I can still visualize him standing there, looking at me for two seconds. Two seconds frozen in time. His helmet in his hand. He had grown a light brown mustache and his hair was a little longer than usual. But that was the end.

I visit his grave often. Not on holidays, but whenever I take a notion I stop by. Each time I experience life all over again. My heart leaps for joy. When Jesus returns Wally will rise out of the ground, soar into the sky, and we will forever be with the Lord (1 Thess. 4:13) .

Death is sometimes called the "unidentified darkness." But

Jesus beat death when He rose from the grave. He beat it for us. It says in the book of John: "I am the resurrection and the life; he who believes in Me will live even if he dies, and everyone who lives and believes in Me will never die" (John 11:25, 26).

The New Testament is full of eyewitnesses who saw Jesus after His death and saw Him rise into heaven with the promise to return in the same way. All the disciples became martyrs for the cause because of their devotion and allegiance to Jesus except for John who was banished to the Isle of Patmos where he wrote the book of Revelation. There's hope in the grave through Jesus.

I know there are many doctrines and philosophies regarding death and the grave, but one thing I do know, nothing will separate us from God: "For I am convinced that neither death, nor life, nor angels, nor principalities, nor things present, nor things to come, nor powers, nor height, nor depth, nor any other created thing, will be able to separate us from the love of God, which is in Christ Jesus our Lord" (Rom. 8:38, 39).

When I was ten years old, I remember watching a movie about a man named Peter Marshall. He was a little before my time, but history tells us that he was the chaplain for the United States Senate in the late 1940s. The movie depicted several of his unusual encounters with God. In fact, the manner in which God called him into the ministry was quite remarkable. He was born in Coatbridge, Scotland, a city that was the chief center of the Scottish iron trade. He had always aspired to be in the British Navy; he did not grow up with a desire to be a minister. However, God had other plans. Peter remained doggedly resolute and did not easily give up his cherished ambition.

All the while God brought people into his life to influence him to no avail. Peter admired Eric Liddell, Scotland's greatest and best-loved athlete, a divinity student whose plan was to be a missionary. We all know this man today because of the movie *Chariots of Fire*. To Peter, he was a hero, not so much because of his athletic ability, but because of his great Christian witness. Eric honored God by refusing unequivocally to run the

100-meter dash, when he discovered the heats were to be held on a Sunday. He decided to train for the 400-meter race even though it was not his area of expertise. Someone slipped a note into his hand just before the race on which was written these words, "Them that honour me I will honour" (1 Sam. 2:30, KJV). Of course, we know Eric established a new world record for the 400-meter dash and a reputation for the greatest quarter-miler yet seen. But more than that, thousands of young people were influenced because of his stand for God, including a young Scotsman named Peter Marshall.

"Walking back from a nearby village to Bamburgh one dark, starless night, Peter struck out across the moors, thinking he would take a short cut. He knew that there was a deep deserted limestone quarry close by the Glororum Road, but he thought he could avoid that danger spot. The night was inky black, eerie. There was only the sound of the wind through the heather-strained moorland, the noisy clamor of wild muir fowl as his footsteps disturbed them, the occasional far-off bleating of a sheep.

"Suddenly he heard someone call, 'Peter!' There was great urgency in the voice.

He stopped. 'Yes, who is it? What do you want?' For a second he listened, but there was no response, only the sound of the wind. The moor seemed completely deserted. Thinking he must have been mistaken, he walked on a few paces. Then he heard it again, even more urgently, 'Peter!'

"He stopped dead still, trying to peer into that impenetrable darkness, but suddenly stumbled and fell to his knees. Putting out his hand to catch himself, he found nothing there. As he cautiously investigated, feeling around in a semicircle, he found himself to be on the very brink of the abandoned stone quarry. Just one step more would have sent him plummeting into space to certain death.

"This incident made an unforgettable impression on Peter. There was never any doubt in his mind about the source of that

Voice. He knew God must have some great purpose for his life to have intervened so specifically. Through subsequent years, there were other close encounters with death, but God always brought him through. He could clearly see God's hand on his life" (Catherine Marshall, *A Man Called Peter,* p. 272).

He knew at that moment God had called his name, saving him from death, but even more, that God was calling him into lifelong service. Not all pastors are called in such a dramatic manner. As history tells us, he lived his entire life serving God and some of it in a high place of honor.

His prayers in the United States Senate, and some of his sermons, were masterpieces that his wife, Catherine Marshall, collected into a book after his death. In the past few years, I've read her books and have been deeply inspired.

Furthermore, she describes the manner in which Peter died. When he was a young forty-six, he sustained a major heart attack. He went by ambulance to the hospital. Catherine was not able to ride with him, for she could not leave their only son alone. She received a phone call at home informing her of his death. The last time she had seen him alive was in her lower hall, just before the ambulance left. The following quotation describe what took place in their final moments together before he passed away, and this is exactly how the film I watched ended. It made quite an impression upon me, and I shed many tears while watching the movie because of her distress. My parents came home from shopping, I was crying so hard they were concerned, but I couldn't speak to explain—it hit me deep and I never forgot it.

"Now I understand those words, 'O memories, that bless and burn,' O God, how it hurts!

"Later that evening, after the tempest of emotion had subsided a bit, I headed beachward. The waves made gentle little lapping noises on the pebbled shore, and there was a path of silver across the water. The crisp sea air fanned my hot cheeks. Suddenly I remembered something, the last words I had ever spoken to Peter. Was it possible that God had prompted those words, seemingly so casual?

"The scene was etched forever on my mind—Peter lying on the stretcher where the two orderlies had put him down for a moment, while the ambulance waited just outside the front door. Peter had looked up at me and smiled through his pain, his eyes full of tenderness, and I had leaned close to him and said, 'Darling, I'll see you in the morning.'

"And as I stood looking out toward that far horizon, I knew that those words would go singing in my heart down all the years" (*Ibid.*, p. 272).

These words were so moving to me that I cried my heart out at the end of the movie. She explained that later God gave her a dream that she would see Peter in heaven some day in the morning, and that the word "morning" was very significant. In her book about his life, she clarifies that to a poet "morning" always means the beginning of something. Poems are an avenue to the deepest feelings that can't be expressed except in rhyme.

Although I don't remember the title of the hymn, the following words have stuck with me and impacted my life. "I am walking with the King, and His praises sweet I sing, ever trav'ling t'ward that City bright and fair, saints before me there have gone, and I'm moving on and on.

"I will never go astray from this blessed holy way. Jesus give me grace and glory here to share, but the greater joys divine in that city shall me mine. Soon the pearly gates I'll see, standing open wide for me, and I'll enter that great city built foursquare, Then with Jesus glorified, safe with loved ones to abide.

"In the morning, in the morning I'll be there, yes, I'll be there. Oh, that city of the blest, where I'll enter into rest! When rejoicing in the morning bright and fair, so bright and fair!

In the morning, in the morning I'll be there, yes, I'll be there."

God knows every detail about us, and He knew that movie would have a profound impression upon me when I was young. Strangely enough, these were the last words Wally ever said to me. I believe they were predestined. They were out of the ordinary, yet so very normal at the time. Nevertheless, these final words will forever comfort me.

My son, Stevie, told me recently that he's never doubted God's existence partly because of what happened to his father. We know God exists and is aware of us personally. If all this had happened without God intervening, I would only have shattered dreams to confess.

Unlike Peter Marshall who gave his life to God when he was young and kept the faith until the end, Wally accepted God when it counted. God demonstrated his love for Wally, who was a good man, but who gave little thought to spiritual matters. He guided and protected him through numerous accidents and hair-raising experiences only to have his life culminate in such a powerful manner. My mind almost explodes as I realize that God loved Wally as much as Peter Marshall. We don't have to be rich, lovely, popular, talented, or famous for God to love us. That took a while to sink in. His love stems from the fact that He made us in His image: "Before I formed you in the womb I knew you, and before you were born I consecrated you" (Jer. 1:5).

God loves us and is capable of total forgiveness of sins. Teaching second grade has given me a comprehensible eyewitness of how children get angry at a friend for a second and forgive them almost instantly. This quality is lost as we become adults, which is to our demise.

"Sing praise to the Lord, you His godly ones, and give thanks to His holy name. For His anger is but for a moment, His favor is for a lifetime; Weeping may last for the night, But a shout of joy comes in the morning" (Ps. 30:4, 5).

I've learned that life is a journey, not a home; a road, not a city of habitation. Enjoyments and blessings are but little inns on the roadside. We get refreshed and move on.

The world tells you to live while you can. Seize the pleasures of the passing day. The preacher cries live while you can and give God each moment as it flies by. My opinion. Let both views unite. I live in pleasure *while* I live for God. "'For I know the plans I have for you,' declares the Lord, 'plans to prosper you and not to harm you, plans to give you hope and a future'" (Jer. 29:11, NIV).

Solomon wrote the book of Ecclesiastes, and it is known to be one of the hardest books for theologians to understand. The author asks lots of questions with no answers. But the book can certainly entice a mind to consider many areas and concepts in life. Nevertheless, the conclusion is an astonishing solution to the meaning of our existence.

In addition to being a wise man, the Preacher also taught the people knowledge; and he pondered, searched out and arranged many proverbs. The Preacher sought to find delightful words and to write words of truth correctly. The words of wise men are like goads, and masters of *these* collections are like well-driven nails; they are given by one Shepherd. But beyond this, my son, be warned: the writing of many books is endless, and excessive devotion *to books* is wearying to the body. The conclusion, when all has been heard, *is*: fear God and keep His commandments, because this *applies to* every person (Eccl. 12:9–13).

We invite you to view the complete
selection of titles we publish at:

www.ASPECTBooks.com

Scan with your mobile
device to go directly
to our website.

Please write or email us your praises, reactions,
or thoughts about this or any other book we publish at:

P.O. Box 954
Ringgold, GA 30736

info@ASPECTBooks.com

ASPECT Books titles may be purchased in bulk for
educational, business, fund-raising, or sales promotional use.
For information, please e-mail:

BulkSales@ASPECTBooks.com

Finally, if you are interested in seeing
your own book in print, please contact us at

publishing@ASPECTBooks.com

We would be happy to review your manuscript for free.

www.ingramcontent.com/pod-product-compliance
Lightning Source LLC
Chambersburg PA
CBHW070543170426
43200CB00011B/2528